626253

D1760487

A Handbook of Case Studies in Finance

A Handbook of Case Studies in Finance

By

Tarika Sikarwar

Cambridge
Scholars
Publishing

A Handbook of Case Studies in Finance

By Tarika Sikarwar

This book first published 2017

Cambridge Scholars Publishing

Lady Stephenson Library, Newcastle upon Tyne, NE6 2PA, UK

British Library Cataloguing in Publication Data
A catalogue record for this book is available from the British Library

ISBN (10): 1-4438-8176-7
ISBN (13): 978-1-4438-8176-0

CONTENTS

Part I

I. Glossary of Terms 3

II. Teaching with Cases included in the Book 21

III. What is a Case Study? 23

IV. Analysing a Case Study 25

V. How to Prepare a Case for Class Discussion 31

VI. Preparing a Written Case Analysis 33

VII. Preparing an Oral Presentation 37

VIII. What is Case Study Analysis? 39

IX. The Role of Financial Analysis in Case Studies 43

Part II

X. Case Studies 51
    1. Hindustan Big Life: Big Problem of Advisors 51
    2. Daily Bharat: A Case of Profitability 54
    3. Financial Crises Setback at Jagat Auto Industry Ltd. 56
    4. Balwinder Finance Case Study 60
    5. Income Tax Case of ABC Oils 63
    6. Diva Life Insurance: A Case of Mis-selling 69
    7. Working Capital Management at Gajraj Oils 73
    8. Max Targets at MAX! 76
    9. Delinquency of Demat Accounts at Rillan 79
    10. EVA Implementation: The Case of Pavitra Group 84
    11. A Case Related to Mishra Ltd. and MDBI Bank 90
    12. Financial Performance: The Case of Saraswati Auto Industries ... 92

13. *Mis-selling: The Case of Parv Money Life Insurance*................... 97

14. *RK Industries: A Case Study on Estimation of Working Capital* 99

15. *JRF Ltd. Case: Inaccurate Sales Forecasting* 106

16. *Financial Fury of Mehta India*.. 108

17. *Avoidable Payment of Interest on Income Tax*............................ 112

18. *A Case Study on Working Capital Loans at IMFC Bank*............. 114

19. *A Case Study on Samachar Rozana Problems Related
    to E.O.Q.* 119

20. *SMT Ltd.: A Case Study on Working Capital Management*......... 124

21. *Sun Light Ltd.: A Case on Capital Budgeting*............................ 127

22. *Big or Small: Financial Loss Matters!*.. 130

23. *Traditional Approach, Limited Promotions: Missed
    Opportunities*.. 132

Teaching Notes.. 135

References 137

PART I

I.

GLOSSARY OF TERMS

Accounts Receivables

Accounts receivable is a legally enforceable claim for payment from a business to its customer/clients for goods supplied and/or services rendered in execution of the customer's order. These are generally in the form of invoices raised by a business and delivered to the customer for payment within an agreed time frame. Accounts receivable is shown on a balance sheet as an asset. It is one of a series of accounting transactions dealing with the billing of a customer for goods and services that the customer has ordered. These may be distinguished from notes receivable, which are debts created through formal legal instruments called promissory notes.

Assets

In financial accounting, an asset is an economic resource. Anything tangible or intangible that can be owned or controlled to produce value and that is considered to have positive economic value is regarded as an asset. Simply stated, assets represent the value of ownership that can be converted into cash (although cash itself is also considered an asset).

Audit

The general definition of an audit is a planned and documented activity performed by qualified personnel to determine by investigation, examination, or evaluation of objective evidence, the adequacy of and compliance with established procedures or applicable documents, and the effectiveness of implementation. The term may refer to audits in accounting, internal controls, quality management, project management, water management, and energy conservation.

Balance Sheet

In financial accounting, a balance sheet or statement of financial position is a summary of the financial balances of a sole proprietorship, a business partnership, a corporation or other business organization, such as an LLC or an LLP. Assets, liabilities and ownership equity are listed as of a specific date, such as the end of its financial year. A balance sheet is often described as a "snapshot of a company's financial condition". Of the three basic financial statements, the balance sheet is the only statement which applies to a single point in time of a business's calendar year.

Bond

In finance, a bond is an instrument of indebtedness from the bond issuer to the holders. It is a debt security, under which the issuer owes the holders a debt and, depending on the terms of the bond, is obliged to pay them interest (the coupon) and/or to repay the principal at a later date, termed the maturity date. Interest is usually payable at fixed intervals (semi-annual, annual, and sometimes monthly). Very often the bond is negotiable, i.e. the ownership of the instrument can be transferred in the secondary market. This means that once the transfer agents at the bank medallion-stamp the bond, it is highly liquid on the secondary market.

CAGR

The year-over-year growth rate of an investment over a specified period of time. The compound annual growth rate is calculated by taking the nth root of the total percentage growth rate, where n is the number of years in the period being considered.

Capital

In economics, capital goods, real capital, or capital assets are already-produced durable goods or any non-financial asset that is used in the production of goods or services.

Capital Budgeting

Capital budgeting (or investment appraisal) is the planning process used to determine whether an organization's long term investments such as new machinery, replacement machinery, new plants, new products, and research development projects are worth the funding of cash through the firm's capitalization structure (debt, equity or retained earnings). It is the process of allocating resources for major capital, investment or expenditures.

Capital Market Instruments

Capital market instruments are responsible for generating funds for companies, corporations and sometimes national governments. These are used by the investors to make a profit out of their respective markets. There are a number of capital market instruments used for market trade, including:

- •Stocks
- •Bonds
- •Debentures
- •Treasury Bills
- •Foreign exchange
- •Fixed deposits, and others

Credit Rating

A credit rating is an evaluation of the credit worthiness of a debtor, especially a business (company) or a government, but not individual consumers. The evaluation is made by a credit rating agency, which examines the debtor's ability to repay the debt and the likelihood of default. Evaluating the creditworthiness of individuals is known as credit reporting and is carried out by credit bureaus or consumer credit reporting agencies, which issue credit scores.

Collateral

In lending agreements, collateral is a borrower's pledge of specific property to a lender, to secure the repayment of a loan. The collateral serves as protection for a lender against a borrower's default—that is, any borrower failing to pay the principal and interest under the terms of a loan obligation. If a borrower does default on a loan (due to insolvency or other event), that borrower forfeits (gives up) the property pledged as collateral, with the lender then becoming the owner of the collateral. In a typical mortgage loan transaction, for instance, the real estate being acquired with the help of the loan serves as collateral. Should the buyer fail to pay the loan under the mortgage loan agreement, the ownership of the real estate is transferred to the bank. The bank uses a legal process called foreclosure to obtain real estate from a borrower who defaults on a mortgage loan obligation. A pawnbroker is an easy and common example of a business that may accept a wide range of items rather than just dealing with cash.

Commodity

In economics, a commodity is a marketable item produced to satisfy wants or needs. Economic commodities are comprised of goods and services.

Debentures

In corporate finance, a debenture is a medium to long-term debt instrument used by large companies to borrow money, at a fixed rate of interest. The legal term "debenture" originally referred to a document that either creates a debt or acknowledges it, but in some countries the term is now used interchangeably with bond, loan stock or note. A debenture is like a certificate of loan or a loan bond evidencing the fact that the company is liable to pay a specified amount with interest and, although the money raised by the debentures becomes a part of the company's capital structure, it does not become share capital. Senior debentures get paid before subordinate debentures, and there are varying rates of risk and payoff for these categories.

Demat Account

In India, shares and securities are held electronically in a dematerialized (or "demat") account, instead of the investor taking physical possession of certificates. A dematerialized account is opened by the investor while registering with an investment broker (or sub-broker). The dematerialized account number is quoted for all transactions to enable electronic settlements of trades to take place. Every shareholder will have a dematerialized account for the purpose of transacting shares. Access to the dematerialized account requires an internet password and a transaction password. Transfers or purchases of securities can then be initiated. Purchases and sales of securities on the dematerialized account are automatically made once transactions are confirmed and completed.

Depository

On the simplest level, depository is used to refer to any place where something is deposited for storage or security purposes. More specifically, it can refer to a company, bank or an institution that holds and facilitates the exchange of securities. A depository can also refer to a depository institution that is allowed to accept monetary deposits from customers.

Depository Participant (DP)

In India, a depository participant (DP) is described as an agent of the depository. They are the intermediaries between the depository and the investors. The relationship between the DPs and the depository is governed by an agreement made between the two under the Depositories Act. In a strictly legal sense, a DP is an entity who is registered as such with SEBI under the sub section 1A of Section 12 of the SEBI Act. As per the provisions of this Act, a DP can offer depository-related services only after obtaining a certificate of registration from SEBI. As of 2012, there were 288 DPs of NSDL and 563 DPs of CSDL registered with SEBI.

Economic Order Quantity (EOQ)

Economic order quantity is the order quantity that minimizes total inventory holding costs and ordering costs. It is one of the oldest classical production scheduling models. The framework used to determine this order quantity is also known as Wilson EOQ Model or Wilson Formula. The model was developed by Ford W. Harris in 1913, but R. H. Wilson, a consultant who applied it extensively, is given credit for his in-depth analysis.

Economic Value Added (EVA)

In corporate finance, EVA is an estimate of a firm's economic profit – being the value created in excess of the required return of the company's investors (being shareholders and debt holders). Quite simply, EVA is the profit earned by the firm, less the cost of financing the firm's capital. The idea is that value is created when the return on the firm's economic capital that is employed, is greater than the cost of that capital. This amount can be determined by making adjustments to GAAP accounting. There are potentially over 160 adjustments that could be made but, in practice, only five or seven key ones are made, depending on the company and the industry in which it competes.

Financial Account

A component of a country's balance of payments that covers claims on or liabilities to non-residents, specifically in regard to financial assets. Financial account components include direct investment, portfolio investment and reserve assets, and are broken down by sector. When recorded in a country's balance of payments, claims made by non-residents on the financial assets of residents are considered liabilities, while claims made against non-residents by residents are considered assets. The financial account differs from the capital account in that the capital account deals with transfers of capital assets. Additionally, the financial account can include claims on land.

Financial Crisis

The term financial crisis is applied broadly to a variety of situations in which some financial assets suddenly lose a large part of their nominal value. In the 19th and early 20th centuries, many financial crises were associated with banking panics, and many recessions coincided with these panics. Other situations that are often called financial crises include stock market crashes and the bursting of other financial bubbles, currency crises, and sovereign defaults. Financial crises directly result in a loss of paper wealth but do not necessarily result in changes in the real economy.

Financial Performance

A subjective measure of how well a firm can use assets from its primary mode of business and generate revenues. This term is also used as a general measure of a firm's overall financial health over a given period of time, and can be used to compare similar firms across the same industry or to compare industries or sectors in aggregation.

Financial Planning

A financial planner or personal financial planner is a professional who prepares financial plans for people. These financial plans often cover cash flow management, retirement planning, investment planning, financial risk management, insurance planning, tax planning, estate planning and business succession planning (for business owners).

Financial Plan

In general usage, a financial plan is a series of steps or goals used by an individual or business, the progressive and cumulative attainment of which is designed to accomplish a financial goal or set of circumstances, e.g. elimination of debt, retirement preparedness, etc. This often includes a budget which organizes an individual's finances and sometimes includes a series of steps or specific goals for spending and saving for the future. This plan allocates future income to various types of expenses, such as rent or utilities, and also reserves some income for short-term and long-term savings. A financial plan is sometimes referred to as an investment plan but, in personal finance, a financial plan can focus on other specific areas such as risk management, estates, college, or retirement.

Financial Ratio

When computing financial ratios and when doing other financial statement analysis always keep in mind that the financial statements reflect the accounting principles. This means assets are generally not reported at their current value. It is also likely that many brand names and unique product lines will not be included among the assets reported on the balance sheet, even though they may be the most valuable of all the items owned by a company.

Financial Service

Financial services are the economic services provided by the finance industry, which encompasses a broad range of organizations that manage money, including credit unions, banks, credit card companies, insurance companies, accountancy companies, consumer finance companies, stock brokerages, investment funds and some government sponsored enterprises.

Forecasting

Forecasting is the process of making statements about events, the actual outcomes of which have not yet been observed. A commonplace example might be the estimation of some variable of interest at some specified future date. Prediction is a similar but more general term. Both might refer to formal statistical methods employing time series, cross-sectional or longitudinal data, or alternatively to less formal judgmental methods. Usage can differ between areas of application. For example, in hydrology, the terms "forecast" and "forecasting" are sometimes reserved for estimates of values at certain specific future times, while the term "prediction" is used for more general estimates, such as the number of times floods will occur over a long period.

Risk and uncertainty are central to forecasting and prediction; it is generally considered good practice to indicate the degree of uncertainty being attached to forecasts. In any case, the data must be up to date in order for the forecast to be as accurate as possible.

Funding

Funding is the act of providing resources, usually in the form of money or other value such as effort or time, for a project, person, business, or any other private or public institution. The process of soliciting and gathering funds is known as fundraising.

Initial Public Offering (IPO)

Initial public offering (IPO), or stock market launch, is a type of public offering where shares of stock in a company are sold to the general public, on a securities exchange, for the first time. Through this process, a private company transforms into a public company. Initial public offerings are used by companies to raise expansion capital, to possibly monetize the investments of early private investors, and to become publicly traded enterprises. A company selling shares is never required to repay the capital to its public investors. After the IPO, when shares trade freely in the open market, money passes between public investors. Although an IPO offers many advantages, there are also significant disadvantages, chief among these are the costs associated with the process and the requirement to disclose certain information that could prove helpful to competitors, or create difficulties with vendors.

Insurance Broking

Insurance is the equitable transfer of the risk of a loss, from one entity to another in exchange for payment. It is a form of risk management primarily used to hedge against the risk of a contingent, uncertain loss.

Insurance Regulatory and Development Authority (IRDA)

The Insurance Regulatory and Development Authority (IRDA) is an autonomous apex statutory body which regulates and develops the insurance industry in India. It was constituted by a Parliament of India act called the Insurance Regulatory and Development Authority Act, 1999, and was duly passed by the Government of India.

Hire Purchase (HP)

Hire purchase (HP), sometimes colloquially known as the "never-never", is the legal term for a contract in which a purchaser agrees to pay for goods in part (or a percentage) over a specified number of months. In Canada and the United States, a hire purchase is termed an instalment plan, although this may differ slightly because in a hire purchase agreement the ownership of the goods remains with the seller until the last payment is made. Other analogous practices are described as closed-end leasing or rent to own.

Just in Time (JIT)

Just in time (JIT) is a production strategy that strives to improve a business's return on investment by reducing in-process inventory and associated carrying costs. Just in time is a type of operations management approach which originated in Japan in the 1950s. It was adopted by Toyota and other Japanese manufacturing firms, with excellent results: Toyota and other companies that adopted the approach ended up significantly raising their productivity through the elimination of waste.

Joint Venture (JV)

A joint venture (JV) is a business agreement in which the parties agree to develop, for a finite time and by contributing equity, a new entity and new assets. They exercise control over the enterprise and consequently share revenues, expenses and assets. There are other types of companies such as JV limited by guarantee and joint ventures limited by guarantee with partners holding shares.

Journal Entry

In accounting, a journal entry is a logging of transactions into an accounting journal. The journal entry can consist of several recordings, each of which is either a debit or a credit. The total of the debits must equal the total of the credits or the journal entry is said to be "unbalanced". Journal entries can record unique items or recurring items such as depreciation or bond amortization. In accounting software, journal entries are usually entered using a separate module from accounts payable, which typically has its own subledger that indirectly affects the general ledger. As a result, journal entries directly change the account balances on the general ledger.

Leasing

A lease is a contractual arrangement calling for the lessee (user) to pay the lessor (owner) for use of an asset. The narrower term, "rental agreement", can be used to describe a lease in which the asset is tangible property. The language that is used in these agreements states that the user "rents" the land or goods that are "let" or "rented out" by the owner. The verb "to lease" is less precise as it can refer to either of these actions. Examples of a lease for intangible property are the use of a computer program (similar to a license, but with different provisions), or the use of a radio frequency (such as a contract with a cell phone provider).

Ledger

A ledger is the principal book or computer file for recording and totalling economic transactions measured in terms of a monetary unit of account by account type. Debits and credits are in separate columns and there is a beginning and ending monetary balance for each account. The term comes from the English dialect forms "liggen" or "leggen", to lie or lay, in sense adapted from the Dutch substantive "legger".

Liquidity Ratios

A class of financial metrics that is used to determine a company's ability to pay off its short-terms debt obligations. Generally, the higher the value of the ratio, the larger the margin of safety that the company possesses to cover short-term debts.

Market Capitalisation

The total dollar market value of all of a company's outstanding shares. Market capitalization is calculated by multiplying a company's outstanding shares by the current market price of one share. The investment community uses this figure to determine a company's size, as opposed to sales or total asset figures.

Merchant Banking

A merchant bank is a financial institution that provides capital to companies in the form of share ownership instead of loans. A merchant bank also provides advice on corporate matters for the firms to which they lend. In the United Kingdom, the term "merchant bank" refers to an investment bank.

Mergers and Acquisitions (M&A)

Mergers and acquisitions (M&A) are both aspects of strategic management, corporate finance and management that deal with the buying, selling, dividing and combining of different companies and similar entities that can help an enterprise to grow rapidly in its sector or location of origin, or in a new field or location, without creating a subsidiary, other child entity or by using a joint venture. Mergers and acquisitions activity can be defined as a type of restructuring in that they result in some entity reorganization with the aim of providing growth or positive value. Consolidation of an industry or sector occurs when widespread M&A activity concentrates the resources of many small companies into a few larger ones, such as occurred with the automotive industry between 1910 and 1940.

Money Market Instruments

As money became a commodity, the money market became a component of the financial markets for assets involved in short-term borrowing, lending, buying and selling, with original maturities of one year or less. Trading in the money markets is done over the counter and is wholesale. Various instruments exist, such as treasury bills, commercial paper, bankers' acceptances, deposits, certificates of deposit, bills of exchange, repurchase agreements, federal funds, and short-lived mortgage and asset-backed securities. It provides liquidity-funding for the global financial system. Money markets and capital markets are parts of the financial markets. The instruments bear differing maturities, currencies, credit risks, and structure. Therefore, they may be used to distribute the exposure.

Mutual Funds

A mutual fund is a type of professionally-managed collective investment scheme that pools money from many investors to purchase securities. While there is no legal definition of the term "mutual fund", it is most commonly applied to those collective investment vehicles that are regulated and sold to the general public. They are sometimes referred to as "investment companies" or "registered investment companies". Most mutual funds are open-ended, meaning stockholders can buy or sell shares of the fund at any time by redeeming them from the fund itself, rather than on an exchange. Hedge funds are not considered a type of mutual fund, primarily because they are not sold publicly.

New Issue

A reference to a security that has been registered, issued and is being sold on a market to the public for the first time. New issues are sometimes referred to as "primary shares" or "new offerings". The term does not necessarily refer to newly-issued stocks, although initial public offerings are the most commonly known new issues. Securities that can be newly-issued include both debt and equity.

Net Operating Profit After Tax (NOPAT)

In corporate finance, net operating profit after tax (NOPAT) is a company's after-tax operating profit for all investors, including shareholders and debt-holders. It is equivalent to earnings before interest after taxes (EBIAT) and equal to NOPLAT. It is defined as follows:

NOPAT = Operating profit x (1 - Tax Rate).

Operating Ratios

A ratio that shows the efficiency of a company's management by comparing operating expense to net sales. Calculated as:

Operating Expense
Net Sales

Portfolio

Any collection of financial assets, such as cash. Portfolios may be held by individual investors and/or managed by financial professionals, hedge funds, banks and other financial institutions. It is a generally accepted principle that a portfolio is designed according to the investor's risk tolerance, time frame and investment objectives. The monetary value of each asset may influence the risk/reward ratio of the portfolio and is referred to as the "asset allocation" of the portfolio.

Primary Market

The primary market is the part of the capital market that deals with issuing new securities. Companies, governments or public sector institutions can obtain funds through the sale of new stock or bond issues through the primary market. This is typically done through an investment bank or finance syndicate of securities dealers.

The process of selling new issues to investors is called underwriting. In the case of a new stock issue, this sale is an initial public offering (IPO). Dealers earn a commission that is built into the price of the security offering, though it can be found in the prospectus. Primary markets create long-term instruments through which corporate entities borrow from the capital market. Once issued, the securities typically trade on a secondary market such as a stock exchange, bond market or derivatives exchange.

Profitability

Profitability is the primary goal of all business ventures. Without profitability, the business will not survive in the long run, so measuring current and past profitability and projecting future profitability is very important. Profitability is measured with income and expenses. Income is money generated from the activities of the business. However, money coming into the business from activities such as borrowing money does not create income; this is simply a cash transaction between the business and the lender to generate cash for operating the business or buying assets. Expenses are the cost of resources used up or consumed by the activities of the business. A resource such as a machine that has a lifespan of more than one year is used up over a period of years. Repayment of a loan is not an expense, but merely a cash transfer, between the business and the lender.

Profitability Ratios

A class of financial metrics that are used to assess a business's ability to generate earnings, compared to its expenses and other relevant costs incurred during a specific period of time. For most of these ratios, having a higher value relative to a competitor's ratio or the same ratio from a previous period is indicative that the company is doing well.

Private Limited

A private limited company is a voluntary association of no less than two and no more than fifty members, whose liability is limited. The transfer of its shares is limited to its members and it is not allowed to invite the general public to subscribe to its shares or debentures.

Public Limited

The standard legal designation of a company which has offered shares to the general public and has limited liability. A public limited company's stock can be acquired by anyone and holders are only limited to potentially lose the amount paid for the shares. It is a legal form more commonly used in the UK. Two or more people are required to form such a company, assuming it has a lawful purpose.

Ratio Analysis

Quantitative analysis of information contained in a company's financial statements. Ratio analysis is based on line items in financial statements, like the balance sheet, income statement and cash flow statement. The ratios of one item – or a combination of items – to another item or combination are then calculated. Ratio analysis is used to evaluate various aspects of a company's operating and financial performance such as its efficiency, liquidity, profitability and solvency. The trend of these ratios over time is studied to check whether they are improving or deteriorating. Ratios are also compared across different companies in the same sector to see how they stack up, and to get an idea of comparative valuations. Ratio analysis is a cornerstone of fundamental analysis.

Regulation

A regulation is a rule or law designed to control or govern conduct. In statist mechanisms it can also be extended to the monitoring and enforcement of rules as established by primary and/or delegated legislation. In this form, it is generally a written instrument containing rules having the force of statist law. Other forms of regulation are self-regulation. In general, regulations are written by executive agencies as a way to enforce laws passed by the legislature.

Return on Assets (ROA)

An indicator of how profitable a company is relative to its total assets. ROA gives an idea of how efficiently management is using its assets to generate earnings. Calculated by dividing a company's annual earnings by its total assets, ROA is displayed as a percentage. Sometimes this is referred to as "return on investment".

The formula for return on assets is: Net Income/Total Assets

Return on Investment (ROI)

Return on investment (ROI) is the concept of an investment of some resource yielding a benefit to the investor. A high ROI means that the investment gains compare favourably to the investment cost. As a performance measure, ROI is used to evaluate the efficiency of an investment or to compare the efficiency of a number of different investments. In purely economic terms, it is one way of considering profits in relation to the capital invested.

Scrap

Scrap consists of recyclable materials left over from product manufacturing and consumption, such as parts of vehicles, building supplies, and surplus materials. Unlike waste, scrap can have significant monetary value.

Secondary Market

The secondary market is also called "aftermarket", and is the financial market in which previously issued financial instruments such as stock, bonds, options, and futures are bought and sold. The secondary market is also used to refer to loans which are sold by a mortgage bank to investors such as Fannie Mae and Freddie Mac. It is further used to refer to the market for any used goods or assets, or an alternative use for an existing product or asset where the customer base is the second market. For example, corn has been used traditionally and primarily for food production and feedstock, but a second or third market has developed for its use in ethanol production.

Shares

In financial markets, a share is a unit of account for various investments. It often means the stock of a corporation, but is also used for collective investments such as mutual funds, limited partnerships, and real estate investment trusts. A corporation divides its capital into shares, which are offered for sale to raise capital, termed as "issuing shares". Thus, a share is an indivisible unit of capital, expressing the ownership relationship between the company and the shareholder. The denominated value of a share is its face value and the total capital of a company is divided into a number of shares. The income received from shares is known as a dividend. A shareholder, also known as a stockholder, is a person who owns shares of a certain company or organization. The process of purchasing and selling shares often involves going through a stockbroker as a middle man.

Seed Capital

The initial capital used to start a business. Seed capital often comes from the company founders' personal assets or from friends and family. The amount of money is usually relatively small because the business is still in the idea or conceptual stage. Such a venture is generally at a pre-revenue stage and seed capital is needed for research and development, to cover initial operating expenses until a product or service can start generating revenue, and to attract the attention of venture capitalists.

Sum Assured

In the case of the maturity of policies that offer no bonus, the sum assured, or a refund of the premium or no money, is receivable by the insured, depending on the type of policy selected. Cover or "death benefit" is the amount of money the nominee receives from the insurance company upon the insured's death.

Surrender Value

The amount payable to a person who surrenders a life insurance policy.

The Securities and Exchange Board (SEBI)

The Securities and Exchange Board of India (SEBI) is the regulator for the securities market in India. It was established in 1988 and given statutory powers on April 12, 1992 through the SEBI Act, 1992.

Term Loan

A term loan is a monetary loan that is repaid in regular payments over a set period of time. Term loans usually last between one and ten years, but can last as long as 30 years in some cases. A term loan usually involves an unfixed interest rate that will add an additional balance to be repaid.

Trading

A trader is a person or entity, in finance, who buys and sells financial instruments such as stocks, bonds, commodities and derivatives, in the capacity of agent, hedger, arbitrageur, or speculator. According to the Wall Street Journal (2004), a managing director convertible bond trader was earning between $700,000 and $900,000, on average.

Venture Capital (VC)

Venture capital (VC) is financial capital provided to early-stage, high-potential growth start-up companies. The venture capital fund earns money by owning equity in the companies in which it invests. This is often a novel technology or business model within the high technology industries, such as biotechnology, IT and software. The typical venture capital investment occurs after the seed funding round, as the first round of institutional capital to fund growth (also referred to as Series A round,) in the interest of generating a return through an eventual realization event, such as an IPO or trade sale of the company. Venture capital is a type of private equity.

Weighted Average Cost of Capital (WACC)

A calculation of a firm's cost of capital in which each category of capital is proportionately weighted. All capital sources – common stock, preferred stock, bonds and any other long-term debt – are included in a WACC calculation. All else being equal, a firm's WACC increases as the beta and rate of return on equity increases, as an increase in WACC notes a decrease in valuation and a higher risk. The WACC equation is the cost of each capital component multiplied by its proportional weight and then summing:

$$WACC = r_D (1 - T_c) * (D/V) + r_E * (E/V)$$

Where...

- r_D = The required return of the firm's Debt financing
- $(1 - T_c)$ = The Tax adjustment for interest expense
- (D/V) = (Debt/Total Value)
- r_E = the firm's cost of equity
- (E/V) = (Equity/Total Value)

Wealth Advisory

Wealth management, as an investment-advisory discipline, incorporates financial planning, investment-portfolio management, and a number of aggregated financial services. High-net-worth individuals (HNWIs), small-business owners and families who desire the assistance of a credentialed financial advisory specialist call upon wealth managers to coordinate retail banking, estate planning, legal resources, tax professionals and investment management. Wealth managers can have backgrounds as independent chartered financial consultants, certified financial planners or chartered financial analysts (in the USA), or chartered strategic wealth professionals (in Canada).

Working Capital Ratio

The working capital ratio (current assets/current liabilities) indicates whether a company has enough short-term assets to cover its short-term debt. Anything below 1 indicates negative W/C (working capital), while anything over 2 means that the company is not investing excess assets. Most believe that a ratio between 1.2 and 2.0 is sufficient. It is also known as "net working capital".

II.

TEACHING WITH CASES INCLUDED IN THE BOOK

All of these case studies are based on real scenarios. The stories have been constructed with data from real organizations collected during visits. All of the cases have open-ended problems. Students tend to prefer to try to find a definitive single solution but, there are none. This book is designed to have the student succeed in applying the theories in real-world situations. They will also see what can be distinct situations in the workplace. Students get to explore multiple perspectives and address the impacts of different decisions.

III.

WHAT IS A CASE STUDY?

A case study presents an account of what happened to a business or industry over a number of years. Cases bring to life the events that managers have to deal with on a day to day basis. Cases enable the student to experience the organizational problems that he or she probably has not had the opportunity to experience first-hand.

Secondly, cases better facilitate the learning of a theory by an individual. The practical application of these better reveal what is going on in real-world companies. This method of teaching facilitates the evaluation of solutions that companies adopted to deal with particular problems.

Thirdly, case studies give students the opportunity to participate in class, as well as gain experience from the presentation of ideas. There are times when a teacher asks a student group to identify what is going on in a case and, through classroom discussion, the issues in and solutions to the problems of the case will reveal themselves. In such instances, students have to organize their views and conclusions so that they are able to present them to the class. Students and teachers will find that, in many instances, even the students' peers may have analysed the issues differently. This facilitates helpful discussions which can lead to a consensus, which may (or may not) be the solution provided by the group to which the assignment was assigned. To that end, student groups are encouraged to prepare well and be prepared to debate potential issues which may arise.

Conversely, there may be instances where cases are assigned to an individual prior to the class taking place. The individual will be responsible for a 30 or 40-minute presentation of the case to the class. In these instances, the individual should try to cover the issues involved and the problems facing the company, and then propose a series of recommendations for resolving the problems.

After the student presents, discussion can be opened up to the class. This facilitates the learning of skills that help to effectively convey ideas to others. Group analysis provides the critical lessons associated with processes involved in working as a team.

IV.

ANALYSING A CASE STUDY

To analyse a case study, students must thoroughly examine the issues with which the company is confronted. This will require the case to be read several times. Once the student has a clear idea of the factual matrix, further efforts can be made to better understand and grasp the specific problems.

Typically, a detailed analysis of a case study may include eight areas:

1. The history, development, and growth of the company over a period of time;
2. Recognition of the company's internal strengths and weaknesses;
3. The temperament of the external environment surrounding the company;
4. A SWOT analysis;
5. The kind of corporate-level strategy pursued by the company;
6. The nature of the company's business-level strategy;
7. The company's structure and control systems, and how they match its strategy; and
8. Recommendations.

To analyse a case, one needs to apply learned concepts to the scenarios raised by the case. Below are the steps one can take to analyse the case material:

Analysis of a company's history, development, and growth

An easy way to investigate how a company's past strategy and structure affect it in the present is to chart the critical incidents which occurred throughout its history. Some events have to be traced from key start-up events, such as the initial product offering and new-product market decisions, as well as how the organization has developed and how it chooses the functional competencies it will pursue.

Identification of a company's internal strengths and weaknesses

This requires carrying out a SWOT analysis. All incidents since the inception of the organization should be used. These must be considered in order to develop an accurate profile of the company's strengths and weaknesses, as they have emerged historically. Additionally, each of the value-creation functions of the company have to be critically identified and analysed to determine current strengths and weaknesses.

Analysis of the external environment

The next step involves detecting the opportunities and threats that are prevalent in the business's environment. This entails an analysis of industry factors and macro environments, to establish the environment that the company is facing. Of great importance at industry level is the use of Porter's five forces model and the stage of the life cycle model. The factors in the macro environment will appear salient depending on the specific company being analysed. However, it is still advisable that each factor (for instance, demographic factors) is used to ascertain whether it is relevant for the company in question.

Completion of this analysis will generate both an analysis of the company's environment and a list of opportunities and threats. The SWOT checklist lists the most common environmental opportunities and threats that one may look for, but the list that is generated will be specific to the company being examined.

Evaluation of the SWOT analysis

After identifying the organization's external opportunities and threats, as well as its internal strengths and weaknesses, the next step is to balance these strengths and weaknesses against the opportunities and threats. The questions that need to be considered specifically relate to the overall strength of the business's competitive position in relation to its ability to continuously pursue its current business or corporate-level strategy profitably; the steps to be taken to turn weaknesses into strengths and threats into opportunities; and the ability to develop new functional, business, or corporate strategies to accomplish the change, and so forth. To that end, it is evident that merely generating the SWOT analysis and then putting it aside will not work. As it gives a brief summary of the company's condition, a good SWOT analysis is the key to all the analyses that follow.

Analysis of corporate-level strategy

In order to carry out the analysis of a company's corporate-level strategy, the company's mission and goals first have to be defined. More often than not, one can find the mission and goals explicitly stated but other times one has to infer what they are from available information. The information required to find out a company's corporate strategy includes the kind of business and the nature of its subsidiaries, mergers and acquisitions. If a company has different business lines, then it is important to analyse the relationship between the company's different businesses. For example: Is there a trade or exchange of resources between them? Are the gains achieved independently or are they achieved through a synergy between or amongst them?

There are other issues to be considered. These include how and why the company's strategy has changed over a period of time. What are the reasons for this change? Does the analysis of the company's businesses or products discover and evaluate the situation and identify which divisions are contributing the most to or detracting from its competitive advantage? It is also useful to gain information from the company's history and explore how the company has built its portfolio over time. Has it acquired any new businesses or ventured its own internally? All of these factors provide clues about the company and indicate ways of improving its future performance.

Analysis of business-level strategy

Once the information has been obtained about the company's corporate-level strategy and the SWOT analysis has been completed, the next step is to identify the company's business-level strategy: whether the company is a single-business company and whether its business-level strategy is identical to its corporate-level strategy. If the company is comprised of many businesses, each business will have its own business-level strategy. One should identify the company's generic competitive strategy, including whether it is differentiation, low cost, or focus strategy, as well as its investment strategy vis-a-vis the company's relative competitive position and the stage of its life cycle. Further, it is possible that the company may also market different products using different business-level strategies. While analysing, one needs to be sure to provide a full account of the company's business-level strategy, to show how it competes.

The SWOT analysis would have already provided information on the company's functional competencies. Further investigation into its marketing, production, or research and development strategy should be carried out to gain a better picture of where the company is going. Another important issue relates to recognition of the functional strategies that a company pursues to build competitive advantage through quality, innovation, superior efficiency, and customer responsiveness, so as to achieve its business-level strategy. For example, if a company is pursuing a low-cost or differentiation strategy successfully, it requires a very different set of competencies. The questions which arise are: Has it developed the right ones? If it has, how can these be further exploited? Can it simultaneously pursue both a low-cost and differentiation strategy?

If the industry analysis (for example, Porter's model), has exposed the threats to the company from the external environment, the SWOT analysis is very important at this juncture. Through analysis, one can find the answers to such considerations as whether or not the company deal with these threats, and how it should change its business-level strategy to counter them.

Once this analysis is complete, one will have a fuller picture of the company's mode of operation and be in a better position to evaluate the potential of the current strategy. One will therefore be able to make recommendations concerning the pattern of the company's future actions. However, at the outset, one needs to consider strategy implementation, or the way the company tries to achieve its strategy.

Analysis of structure and control systems

The reason for this analysis is to identify which structure the company is using to implement its strategy. It also determines which methods are best for evaluating whether that structure is the most appropriate one for the company. Different corporations and business strategies require different structures. For instance, does the company have the right level of vertical differentiation (does it have the right number of levels in the hierarchy or decentralized control)? Or, does it have horizontal differentiation (does it use a functional structure when it should be using a product structure)? Similarly, it is also necessary to analyse whether the company is using the right mix, as well as control systems, to manage its operations. One also has to consider factors such as whether or not managers are being adequately rewarded, and if the right rewards are in place to encourage cooperation between divisions. These are all issues to be considered.

In some cases, there will be little information, whereas in others there will be a lot of information on these aspects. Nonetheless, in analysing each case one should gear the analysis towards its most salient issues. For instance, organizational conflict, power, and politics may be important issues for some companies. Try to analyse and find out reasons why the problems in these areas are occurring. Are they occurring because of bad strategy formulation or because of bad strategy implementation?

Because the companies are attempting to alter their strategies or structures to solve strategic problems, organizational change is a relevant subject in many cases. So, as a part of the analysis, one may suggest a course of action that the company in question could use to achieve its goals. For example, one may come up with a list of the steps the company would follow to alter its business-level strategy from differentiation to focus.

Making recommendations

The final part of the case analysis process involves making recommendations based on the analysis. Evidently, the quality of the recommendations is a direct result of the meticulousness with which one has prepared the case analysis. The work one has put into the case analysis will be noticeable to the faculty from the nature of the recommendations. Recommendations are directed at solving whatever strategic problem the company is facing as well as increasing its future profitability. The recommendations should be in line with the analysis. In other words, they should logically follow on from the previous discussion. For instance, the recommendation will generally centre on the exact methods of changing functional, business, and corporate strategy, as well as organizational structure and control to improve the business's performance. The set of recommendations will be specific to each case. For instance, the recommendations may include the divesting of businesses, a change from a strategy of unrelated to related diversification, an increase in spending on specific research and development projects, an increase in the level of integration among divisions by using task forces and teams, or a move to a different kind of structure to implement a new business-level strategy. Again, one has to make sure that the recommendations are mutually consistent and are written in the form of an action plan. The plan might contain a timetable that itemises the actions for changing the company's strategy and a description of how changes at corporate level will necessitate business-level changes and, subsequently, functional-level changes.

After following all of the above-mentioned stages and performing a thorough analysis of the case, the resulting ideas can be presented to the class and discussion can be encouraged. Analysis should be tailored to suit the specific issue discussed in the case. In some cases, there may be the flexibility to completely omit one of the steps in the analysis because it may not be relevant to the specific situation under consideration. One must be sensitive to the needs of the case and apply the steps accordingly. The framework is only a guide and not an outline that one must use to do a successful analysis.

V.

HOW TO PREPARE A CASE
FOR CLASS DISCUSSION

1. Scan the case quickly to get an overview of the situation it presents.
This quick overview gives a general picture of the situation and indicates the kinds of issues and problems an individual may come across while solving the case. Next, one has to proceed with study questions for the case.

2. Thoroughly read the case to understand the facts and circumstances.
While reading the case, one should try to gain full command of the situation it presents and then start to develop some tentative answers to the questions.

3. Carefully review all the information presented in the annexure and exhibits.
Often, the information in the numbers contained in the exhibits is crucial enough to materially affect the diagnosis of the situation.

4. Decide what the strategic issues are in the case.
After identifying the strategic issues and problems in the case, the next step is to analyse which tools and analytical techniques are to be used. Many times the strategic issues are clear but at other times one has to dig them out from all the information given.

5. Begin analysis of the issues with some number-crunching.
Most finance cases call for some kind of number-crunching or calculation of assorted financial ratios to ascertain the following: the company's financial condition and recent performance; a calculation of the growth rates of sales or profits or unit volume; the profit margins and the make-up of the cost structure; the revenue cost-profit relationships that are present.

6. Apply the concepts and techniques of financial analysis.
Financial analysis is not just a collection of opinions but also entails the application of concepts and analytical tools to go beneath the surface to produce sharp insight and understanding.

7. Support the diagnosis and opinions with reasons and evidence.
It is important to prepare answers to the question, "why?" In other words, find concrete reasons for choosing the answer in order to effectively support it.

8. Develop an appropriate action plan and set of recommendations.
The good manager is always to convert sound analysis into sound actions—actions that will produce the desired results. Hence, the final and most telling step in preparing a case is to develop an action agenda for management that lays out a set of specific recommendations on what to do.

VI.

PREPARING A WRITTEN CASE ANALYSIS

Preparing a written case analysis is similar to preparing a case for class discussion. The analysis must be more complete and should be presented in the form of a report which should focus on the following points:

(1) Identifying all the important issues that should be addressed by management;
(2) Performing an appropriate analysis (analysis and evaluation);
(3) Proposing an action plan and set of recommendations that address the issues identified in the case.

Analysis and Evaluation

Analysis and evaluation are considered to be the toughest aspects of writing the report. The firm's financial ratios, profit margins and rates of return, and capital structure all need to be thoroughly checked and a decision made about how strong the firm is financially.

Marketing, production, managerial competence, and other aspects underlying the organization's success and failures should be looked at and, based on this, a decision made about whether the firm has valuable resource strengths and competencies and if it is capitalizing on them.

In writing the analysis and evaluation, bear in mind four things, as quoted by Thompson and Strickland in *Strategic Management: Concepts and Cases* (10th edition):

1. "You are obliged to offer analysis and evidence to back up your conclusions. Do not rely on unsupported opinions, over-generalizations and platitudes as a substitute for tight, logical argument backed up with facts and figures".

2. *"If your analysis involves some important quantitative calculations, use tables and charts to present the calculations clearly and efficiently. Don't just tack the exhibits on at the end of your report and let the reader figure out what they mean and why they were included. Instead, in the body of your report cite some of the key numbers, highlight the conclusions to be drawn from the exhibits, and refer the reader to your charts and exhibits for more details".*

3. *"Demonstrate that you have command of the strategic concepts and analytical tools to which you have been exposed. Use them in your report".*

4. *"Your interpretation of the evidence should be reasonable and objective. Be wary of preparing a one-sided argument that omits all aspects not favourable to your conclusions. Likewise, try not to exaggerate or overdramatize. Endeavour to inject balance into your analysis and to avoid emotional rhetoric. Strike phrases such as 'I think,' 'I feel,' and 'I believe' when you edit your first draft and write in 'My analysis shows,' instead".*

Recommendations

The last section of the written analysis should consist of recommendations, as well as a plan of action. The recommendations ought to address all of the identified and analysed problems/issues in the case. It should be made clear how the recommendations will help solve the problems that have been identified. Again, ensure that the recommendations are practical and the company is financially able to carry out whatever is recommended. Recommendations are considered workable when there is an acceptance of the people involved and the organization is competent to implement them in the given market and environmental constraints.

Recommendations should be made with detail and specificity. Only then can they be meaningful. One should evade unhelpful absurd statements such as, "more planning is required" or "aggressive marketing of product is required."

1. Do not repeat, in summary form, large pieces of factual information from the case. The instructor has read the case and knows what is going on. Rather, use the information in the case to illustrate your statements, defend your arguments and make salient points. Beyond the brief introduction to the company, you must avoid being descriptive and instead be analytical.

2. Make sure that the sections and subsections of your discussion flow logically and smoothly from one to the next. That is, try to build on what has gone before so that the analysis of the case study moves towards a climax. This is particularly important for group analysis, because there is a tendency for people in a group to split up the work and say, "I'll do the beginning, you take the middle, and I'll do the end." The result is a choppy, stilted analysis because the parts do not flow from one to the next, and it is obvious to the instructor that no real group work has been done.

3. Avoid grammatical and spelling errors. They make the paper sloppy.

4. In some instances, cases dealing with well-known companies don't include up-to-date research because it was not available at the time the case was written. If possible, do a search for more information on what has happened to the company in subsequent years. The following are sources of information for performing this search:

(a) The World Wide Web is the place to start your research. Very often you can download copies of a company's annual report from its website. Many companies also keep lists of press releases and articles that have been written about them. Thoroughly search the company's website for information such as the company's history and performance, and download all relevant information at the beginning of your project.

(b) Compact disc sources such as Lotus One Source and InfoTrac provide an amazing amount of good information, including summaries of recent articles written on specific companies that you can then access in the library.

- F&S Predicates provide an annual listing of all the articles written about a particular company. Simply reading the titles gives an indication of what has been happening in the company.
- Annual reports on a Form 10-K often provides an organization chart.
- Companies themselves provide information if you write and ask for it.
- Fortune, Business Week, and Forbes have many articles on companies featured in most cases.
  Standard and Poor's industry reports provide detailed information about the competitive conditions facing the company's industry. Be sure to look at this journal.

- Sometimes instructors provide questions for each case to help with analysis. These often illuminate the important issues that have to be covered in the discussion and should be used as a guide for writing the case analysis.
- If you follow the guidelines in this section, you should be able to write a thorough and effective evaluation.

VII.

PREPARING AN ORAL PRESENTATION

Both oral presentations and written analysis require identification of the issues and problems that are confronting the organization. In addition, there must be an investigation into industry conditions and the company's situation, and the development of a systematic, well-reasoned action plan.

The matter of analysis and the quality of recommendations in an oral presentation should be the same as in a written report. In common with a written assignment, one needs to display a commanding authority over the relevant concepts and tools of analysis, and the recommendations should contain all the detail needed to provide clear-cut direction for management. The difference between an oral presentation and a written case lies in the delivery format. Oral presentations rely primarily on verbalizing the diagnosis, analysis, and recommendations and visually enhancing and supporting the oral discussion with colourful, snappy slides. Usually, oral presentations involve group assignments.

A good set of slides with good content and good visual appeal is essential to a first-rate presentation. Take some care in choosing a suitable slide design, font size and style, and colour scheme. The slides may cover each of the following areas:

- An opening slide covering the title of the presentation and names of the presenters.
- A slide showing an outline of the presentation.
- One or more slides covering the key problems and strategic issues that the decision-maker needs to address.
- A series of slides covering the analysis of the company's situation.
- A series of slides containing the recommendations, the supporting arguments, and the reasoning behind each recommendation. One slide for each recommendation and the associated reasoning has a lot of merit.

Carefully plan and practice the slideshow to make best use of impact and to minimize distractions. The slideshow should contain all of the ingredients required to garner the attention of the audience, but not too many points to distract from the main elements of what group members are saying to the class. One should remember that the job of slides is to help communicate the points to the audience.

Too much use of graphics, figures, images, colours, and transition effects may divert the attention of the audience away from what is being said.

VIII.

WHAT IS CASE STUDY ANALYSIS?

A case study is the presentation of incidents that have occurred in relation to a business, organization or industry over a period of time. It records the events that managers have had to deal with, such as changes in the competitive environment, and charts the managers' responses, which have usually involved changing the business- or corporate-level strategy.

Case studies are valuable in diverse fields, courses and specializations for many reasons. Firstly, cases offer the student experience of organizational problems that they probably have not had the opportunity to experience first-hand. In a relatively short period of time, students will have the chance to appreciate and analyse the problems faced by many different companies and to understand how managers tried to deal with them.

Secondly, cases are illustrations of what has been learned. The theory and concepts help to disclose what is going on in the company and allow the solutions that specific companies adopted to be evaluated. Therefore, during the analysis of the cases, the student effectively becomes an investigating detective who, by using a set of conceptual tools, probes what has happened in the case and what or who was responsible. In addition, after investigation, the evidence is marshalled and a solution is provided. In this exercise, top managers also enjoy the adventure of testing their problem-solving abilities in the real world. It is important to remember that no one knows what the right answer is for the situation. All that managers (students) can do is to make the best assumptions. We are all aware that management is an uncertain game; using cases to see how theory can be put into practice is one way of improving one's skills of diagnostic investigation.

Thirdly, case studies give students the opportunity to participate in class and to gain experience in presenting their ideas to others. Teachers may sometimes call on students as a group to find out what is going on in a case and, through classroom discussion, facilitate the uncovering of the issues and solutions. In such situations, students have to organize their views and conclusions so that they can present them to the class. The other colleagues may have analysed the same issues differently and may want to hear justified arguing of the points before they accept the conclusions. Students should therefore be prepared for debate. This is how decisions are made in the actual business world.

Teachers may ask an individual student or group to evaluate the case before the class. The individual or the group may prepare a 15 or 20-minute presentation of the case to the class. The presentation must cover the issues involved and the problems faced by the company, in addition to a series of recommendations for resolving the problems. The discussion can be further thrown open to the class and the presenter will have to defend the ideas. During such discussions and presentations, students learn how to effectively convey their thoughts and ideas to others. One must bear in mind that managers spend a lot of time in situations like these as they present and discuss with other managers the current and future challenges. A student is thus able to experience in the classroom the reality of what goes on in a business setting, and this will help provide experience for a future career.

While analysing the case studies in groups, students also learn about the group process involved in working as a team. When students work in groups, they develop the skill of scheduling time and allocating responsibilities, even though these are always difficult as some members will shirk their responsibilities and only a few will be dominant. However, these are practical issues that one has to face when working in organizations and, as such, it is imperative that the attributes and skills that are needed to succeed in this environment are nurtured.

The Ten Commandments of Case Analysis

Compiled below are a few steps to help in case analysis and in preparing a case for written as well as oral presentation.

1. Read the case twice. Once as a quick overview and the second time in detail to gain full knowledge of the facts. All information should be accounted for, including what is present in exhibits.
2. List the problems and issues identified in the case and what the management needs to address.
3. Do a thorough analysis of the company's current situation.

4. Find out likely opportunities where the concepts and analytical tools that have been studied theoretically can be practically applied.
5. Do an adequate number of ups and downs. Read and re-read the case to discover the hidden story.
6. Support your answers/opinion with the supporting evidence given in the case. Even the numerical data (if given) can be used in support of any conclusion.
7. Write down the recommendations in the order of their feasibility and acceptability within the given timespan.
8. Support suggestions/recommendations with reasons. These should be sensible and likely to result in an improvement of the company's performance.
9. Review again the suggested action plan to see whether it addresses the problems and issues of concern.
10. Avoid giving a recommendation which may have disastrous consequences if it is not planned and worked upon properly. Do think about negative and positive aspects of the same.

IX.

THE ROLE OF FINANCIAL ANALYSIS
IN CASE STUDIES

The most important facet of analysing a case study and writing the analysis is the role and use of financial information. A cautious analysis of the company's financial position and condition immensely improves a case write-up. Financial data represents the results of the path and strategy that the company is following. Although analysing financial statements is pretty complex, a general idea of a company's financial position and wellbeing can be determined through the use of ratio analysis.

Financial ratios are classified into five different categories: profit ratios, liquidity ratios, activity ratios, leverage ratios, and shareholder-return ratios. Calculation of financial performance ratios is done from the balance sheet and income statement. These ratios of the organization can be compared with the industry average or the company's previous years of performance. It should be understood that deviation from the industry average is not essentially bad; it simply warrants further investigation. In addition to ratio analysis, a company's cash flow and fund flow position is of critical importance and should be assessed. Cash flow shows how much actual cash a company possesses.

Profit Ratios

A class of financial ratios that are used to measure a business's ability to generate earnings, as compared to its expenses and other relevant costs incurred during a specific period of time. Mostly, having a higher value (i.e. a higher value of ratio relative to a competitor's ratio) or having the same ratio from a previous period, is indicative that the company is doing well. It also measures the efficiency of an organization's effective use of resources. A variety of profit ratios can be used. Each type of profitability ratio measures a different facet of a company's performance. The most commonly used profit ratios are gross profit margin, net profit margin, return on total assets, and return on stockholders' equity.

1. **Gross profit margin**. The gross profit margin shows the percentage of sales available to cover general and administrative expenses and other operating costs. It is defined as follows:

Gross Profit Margin =   Sales Revenue - Cost of Goods Sold
                               Sales Revenue

2. **Net profit margin**. Net profit margin is represented as the percentage of profit earned on sales. This ratio is considered important as businesses need to make a profit in order to survive in the long run. It is defined as follows:

Net Profit Margin =   Net Income
                             Sales Revenue

3. **Return on total assets**. This ratio calculates the profit earned on the employment of assets. It is defined as follows:

Return on Total Assets=   Net Income Available to Common Stockholders
                                  Total Assets

Net income is actually the profit earned after preferred dividends (those set by contract) have been paid. Total assets include both current and non-current assets.

4. **Return on stockholders' equity.** This ratio talks about the percentage of profit earned on common stockholders' investment in the company. As per theory, a company should attempt to maximize the wealth of its stockholders and should maximize this ratio. It is defined as follows:

Return on Stockholders' Equity =
                    Net Income Available to Common Stockholders
                    Stockholders' Equity

Liquidity Ratios

The ratio measures an organization's ability to meet short-term obligations. An asset is deemed liquid if it can be readily converted into cash. Liquid assets include current assets such as cash, marketable securities, accounts receivable, and so on. Most commonly used liquidity ratios are current ratio and quick ratio.

1. **Current ratio.** The current ratio measures the degree to which the claims of short-term creditors are covered by assets that can be quickly converted into cash. The ideal ratio that most companies should have is a ratio of at least 1, because failure to meet these commitments can lead to bankruptcy. The ratio is defined as follows:

Current Ratio =   Current Assets/Current Liabilities

2. **Quick ratio.** The quick ratio measures a company's ability to pay off the claims of short-term creditors with its most liquid assets without relying on the sale of its inventories. It is defined as follows:

Quick Ratio = $\dfrac{\text{Current Assets} - \text{Inventory}}{\text{Current Liabilities}}$

Activity Ratios

Activity ratios indicate a company's ability to convert the inside balance sheet into cash/sales, and how well a company administers its assets. Inventory turnover and days sales outstanding (DSO) are particularly useful:

1. **Inventory turnover.** This measures how many times a company's inventory is sold and replaced over a period. It is useful in deciding whether a firm is carrying excess stock in its inventory. It is defined as follows:

Inventory Turnover = Cost of Goods Sold/Inventory

Cost of goods sold is comparatively a better measure of turnover than sales. Some companies compute average inventory as input but, for simplicity, use the inventory at the balance sheet date.

2. **Days sales outstanding (DSO), or average collection period.** This ratio shows the average time an organization has to wait before receiving the cash after making a sale. It measures how effective the company's credit, billing, and collection procedures are. It is defined as follows:

$$DSO = \frac{\text{Accounts Receivable}}{\text{Total Sales}/360}$$

Numerically, accounts receivable is divided by the average daily sales. The use of 360 is a standard number of days for most financial analysis.

Leverage Ratios

A highly leveraged firm is one which uses more debt than equity (including stock and retained earnings). The optimal capital structure has an optimal combination of debt and equity and is determined by the individual company. Three commonly used leverage ratios are debt-to-assets ratio, debt-to-equity ratio, and times-covered ratio.

1. **Debt-to-assets ratio.** The debt-to-asset ratio is the direct measure of the extent to which borrowed funds have been used to finance a company's investments. It is defined as follows:

Debt-to-Assets Ratio = Total Debt/ Total Assets

Total debt is the sum of a company's current liabilities and its long-term debt, and total assets are the sum of fixed assets and current assets.

2. **Debt-to-equity ratio.** The debt-to-equity ratio indicates the relative proportion of shareholders' equity and debt used to finance a company's assets.

It is defined as follows:

Debt-to-Equity Ratio = Total Debt/Total Equity

3. **Times Interest-covered ratio.** This ratio deals with the degree to which a company's gross profit covers its annual interest payments. If the times-covered ratio should never be less than 1, and it is less than 1, it indicates that the company is not able to meet its interest costs. The ratio is defined as follows:

Times-Covered Ratio = Profit Before Interest and Tax/Total Interest Charges

Shareholder-Return Ratios

Shareholder-return ratios indicate the return earned by shareholders from holding stock in a company. The commonly used ratios are total shareholder returns, price-earnings ratio, market to book value and dividend yield.

1. **Total shareholder returns.** Total shareholder returns measure the performance of the company over a period of time. It includes both dividend payments and capital appreciation in the value of the stock (adjusted for stock splits) and is defined as follows:

$$\text{Total Shareholder Returns} = \frac{\text{Stock Price } (t+1)\text{ -Stock Price } (t) + \text{Sum of Annual Dividends per Share}}{\text{Stock Price } (t)}$$

2. **Price-earnings ratio.** An equity multiple valuation. The price-earnings ratio also indicates the amount investors are willing to pay per rupee/dollar of profit. It is defined as follows:

Price-Earnings Ratio = Market Price per Share/Earnings per Share

3. **Market to book value.** This ratio is used to measure the value of a company by comparing the book value of a firm to its market value. It is defined as follows:

Market to Book Value = Market Price per Share/ Earnings per Share

4. **Dividend yield.** The dividend yield measures the return that shareholders received in the form of dividends. It is defined as follows:

Dividend Yield = Dividend per Share/Market Price per Share

A financial ratio that shows how much a company pays out in dividends each year, relative to its share price. Companies with strong growth prospects should have a lower dividend pay-out ratio than mature companies.

PART II

X.

CASE STUDIES

1. Hindustan Big Life: Big Problem of Advisors

The Hindustan Group comprises over 90 operating companies in seven business sectors: communications and information technology; engineering; materials; services; energy; consumer products; and chemicals. The Group has operations in more than 80 countries across six continents, and its companies export products and services to 85 countries. The total revenue of Hindustan companies taken together was $83.5 billion (around Rs 380, 663 crores) in 2010-11, with 57.8% of this coming from business outside India. Hindustan companies employ over 425,000 people worldwide. The Hindustan name has been respected in India for 140 years for its adherence to strong values and business ethics. Every Hindustan company or enterprise operates independently. Each of these companies has its own board of directors and shareholders to whom it is answerable. There are 28 publicly listed Hindustan enterprises and they have a combined market capitalization of about $74.15 billion (as of October 5, 2011), and a shareholder base of 3.5 million. The major Hindustan companies are Hindustan Steel, Hindustan Motors, Hindustan Consultancy Services (TCS), Hindustan Power, Hindustan Chemicals, Hindustan Global Beverages, Indian Hotels and Hindustan Communications.

Hindustan Big Life Insurance Company Limited (Hindustan Big Life) is a joint venture company, formed by Hindustan Sons and AIA Group Limited (AIA). Hindustan Big Life combines Hindustan's pre-eminent leadership position in India and AIA's presence as the largest independent listed pan-Asia life insurance group in the world, spanning 15 markets in Asia Pacific. Hindustan Sons holds a majority stake (74%) in the company and AIA holds 26% through an AIA Group company. Hindustan Big Life Insurance Company Limited was licensed to operate in India on February 12, 2001 and started operations on April 1, 2001.

One of the branches of Hindustan Big Life is located in the Gwalior region of Madhya Pradesh. The case provides some shocking insight, which came after having an interaction with the Branch Manager. Although Hindustan Big operates with a broader vision to meet the lifetime insurance needs of the people, growing competition in the Indian insurance sector (with the entry of private players after the liberalization of the sector) caused alarm in the organization. To effectively deal with the competition, the company focused on spreading their marketing network all over the nation. Similar efforts were made by Mr Dharmendra Singh Chauhan, the SDM for Hindustan Big. He appointed a group of business development managers (BDMs) so that Hindustan Big could reach every nook and cranny of the region and face the heat of competition effectively. But unfortunately the strategy didn't work. There were many aspects which were not considered. Hindustan Big spent large amounts of money on the recruitment and training of advisors and BDMs so that they could have the best manpower at work and, in turn, generate greater business. Other aspects were given adequate attention, though.

However, the role of agents still needed to be addressed in order to attract customers for a "tactful" company. Insurance products, as well as tactful schemes, are "sold and not bought", so only a few would buy the tactful products on a voluntary basis. It is for this reason that so many tactful operators still appoint an agent to attract and convince customers to buy tactful products. To convince the customer, an agent should have high levels of confidence, strong communication skills (persuasiveness), understand what to do (initiating structure), comprehend customer needs, meet customer demands (consideration), and so forth. In this study, tactful agents were surveyed regarding their leadership behaviour. Initiating structure, consideration, representation and persuasiveness were all positively related to the performance of the tactful industry.

The expenditures incurred in recruitment and training did not see commensurate returns. The advisors failed to source sufficient business for the organization and, for the most part, were unable to fulfil the targets given to them. As time passed, the expenditure spent on acquiring and training became greater than the returns' total income. This adversely affected the expenditure account and began to be considered as a weakness of the branch. When the monthly report of the income and expenditures were sent to headquarters, the finance department pressurized them to bring in good business and maintain a balance between income and expenditure. However, this only served to further aggravate the problem.

The result was that a few BDMs started appointing fake advisors so that their own targets could be met.

Hindustan Big is one of the largest diversified financial services institutions in the world and offers a wide range of insurance, investment, healthcare, and asset management products to millions of customers. It is internationally recognized for achieving market strength in its primary businesses through its quality manpower. But the SD manager of the Gwalior region is in a dilemma and the question becomes, how should he proceed?

Questions:

1. Around which organization does the case revolve?
2. What is the main issue in the case?
3. What criteria should be fixed for the appointment of advisors?
4. What is the role of IRDA in this case?
5. Suggest few solutions to the problems of the organization.

2. Daily Bharat: A Case of Profitability

Daily Bharat is an Indian Hindi-language daily newspaper published by D B Corp Ltd. It was started in 1958 from the Indore city of Madhya Pradesh. The newspaper was launched to fulfil the need for a Hindi language daily newspaper; it had the name Savere in Bhopal, and Good Morning All in Gwalior. In 1957 it was renamed the India Samachar and, in 1958 it was renamed again, this time as the Daily Bharat. It now enjoys widespread circulation in India and is actually ranked 1st in India and 11th worldwide for the largest circulation of a daily newspaper. The Daily Bharat displaced Nanhiduniya from Jaipur (in 1995) with 50,000 copies, and the Tribune from Chandigarh (in 2000) with 19,000 copies on the very first day of its launch. The Daily Bharat has a circulation of more than 3.5 million across six states.

When the organization planned to start its Chandigarh edition, it looked to buy a property in the Panchkula suburb because it would have been economical and would have suited their needs. However, during the course of a discussion with a reader from Chandigarh, it came to be known that if the organization wanted readers to perceive the paper to be as prestigious as the Tribune, it would have to operate from an imposing building in the centre of the town and not the outskirts. This caused them to rethink their original ideas and, in the end, they invested in an Rs 3.5 crore (Rs 35 million) property in the city centre, rather than the Rs 50 lakh (Rs 5 million) they had actually planned. This extra investment ensured that people perceived it as a Chandigarh paper right from day one and not just as any other newspaper.

From the financial accounts of company, it can be seen that sales of the Daily Bharat were continuously diminishing, i.e. from 62.06 (March 2004) to 57.34 (March 2008). The biggest reason could be the rise in competition, as opposed to rapid increases, i.e. 5,330 (2005-06), 6,754 (2006-07), 8,627 (2007-08). According to the consolidated financial statements issued by the company (balance sheet, 2008-09), DB owned a share capital of Rs. 1,688 million and NCA of Rs. 6,471 million with investments of Rs. 238 million.

Print media is always a better medium for advertising. Other organizations always use newspapers to promote their companies, brands and products. These advertisement deals are sealed through various channels. Some fraudulent practices by advertising agencies hampered the recovery of

These events were so sudden that no one was prepared for such a rapid decline in the economic cycle across the world. The signs of slowdown were also visible in the business from the second quarter (July-Sept 2008), as sales came down to Rs. 158.51 crores. The situation became worse in the third quarter (October-December 2008), as the company's sales sharply came down to Rs. 78.42 crores. February and March's demand provided a glimpse of hope and revival and, in the fourth quarter, sales rose to Rs. 110.48 crores.

Cumulative sales for the year 2008-09 were Rs. 513.78 crores and net loss was Rs. 16.39 crores. Production of commercial vehicles (CVs) and multi-utility vehicles (MUVs) declined by 35% in 2008-2009 at 637,000 vehicles.

The sudden and unprecedented decline in production and sales from mid-September 2008 until January 2009 adversely impacted the company's financial performance. The management thus took a number of steps to combat the slowdown. These included improving the manpower productivity, as well as that of machinery and available resources, a reduction in wastage and cost reduction, and detection and plugging of all revenue leakages. All the capital expenditures were kept on hold. The company decided to increase its share in the domestic and export replacement markets.

Questions:

1. Which organization is in the picture? Give a brief overview of it.
2. What is a financial crisis?
3. What is the impact of a crisis on the sales and profits?
4. What are the measures that the organization has taken?

4. Balwinder Finance Case Study

In the case of Balwinder Auto and Balwinder Finance Services of Gwalior, the problem was related to their loan products and their customers' lack of awareness. The case was discussed with the Managing Director of Gupta & Sons and they helped to meet with the loan approval department. They discussed the problem and presented the case study for approval.

Introduction of Balwinder Finance Ltd

Incorporated in 1987, Balwinder Finance Limited is one of the most diversified non-banking finance companies (NBFC) in the market, catering to more than 5 million customers across the country. Apart from being a well-recognized organization, the company holds the highest credit rating of FAAA/Stable for any NBFC in the country today. Its product offerings include consumer durable loans, personal loans, cross selling, loans against property, small business loans, home loans, construction equipment loans and loans against securities.

The company has a widespread presence as one of the largest retail financing companies in India, having a network of over 2000 consumer durable partners serviced through more than 70 locations. Its rich experience of over 24 years in consumer finance has satisfied over 4.6 million customers.

Balwinder Finance traditionally had a decentralized application architecture model. This was previously conducive as the company's business operating model was also decentralized. To achieve better control, it implemented centralized application architecture. However, as the company launched a series of new financial products, it required platforms for centralized data aggregation which would enable management to deliver benefits to all stakeholders, including metrics-driven decision-making by management, critical information sharing with customers and partners, and increased communication and collaboration between employees. The company decided to invest in a data warehouse and portal platform, along with a messaging and collaboration platform.

Balwinder Auto Finance Limited is an asset finance company, financing consumer durables, personal and bike loans, small business loans, loans against property and loans against shares. It is an NBFC company.

Challenges

In order to achieve customer satisfaction, Balwinder Finance Services moved to a single platform in order to serve customers well and be better able to drive the loan product within the agency, where customers purchase the product and can connect with the Balwinder Finance loan back office. In the consumer durable business, customers typically choose to pay by cash, credit card or in loan instalments. Generally, transactions are through cash and credit card, bearing in mind that it is desirable for the customer to be able to complete with ease.

Presently, senior customers are moving towards credit card purchases or cash payments because they do not want to take out loans for consumer durable goods. However, Balwinder was planning to build a strong campaign to target customers with a good payment record; the company was preparing this campaign to extend the personal loan offers available to those customers.

Loan officers at Balwinder collected paper-based loan applications and supporting documentation, scanned them, and sent the images to a central operations team for booking and document- verification. If passed, the file was sent to a central credit team for loan approval. The process became messier when incomplete applications or a lack of supporting documents forced the central operations team to send back applications. This happened fairly often as its maximum business comes from customers in Tier-III cities and rural areas where obtaining documents for collateral, like a land agreement, is difficult.

To be more customer-friendly, the organization was coming up with a single system for loan approval so that the headache of managing both the back and front office functions could be minimized. For example, being able to obtain a 30 Lakh loan within 3 hours and in three easy steps.

So, the company wanted to automate the initial processing of loan applications. The bank had some effective indicators of bad risks and wanted to use these criteria to eliminate unsuitable applicants. Information given by each applicant would be screened, using a rule set based on the company's criteria, with the result being a straightforward accept/reject decision on the loan, or a referral for further investigation if the information given by the applicant was not sufficient to reach a decision.

Although the company thought it was the right strategy, it unfortunately proved problematic for customers who previously had a bad track record in their financial obligations. Also, stringent norms proved painful for customers not fulfilling the minimum requirement for loan approval.

Questions:

1. To which area does the case belong?
2. What is the problem in the case?
3. What should the company do in this case?

5. Income Tax Case of ABC Oils

ABC Oils Limited is a leading Indian FMCG company in the edible oil market. ABC Oils has near to 3000 employees spread over its 7 manufacturing plants, marketing offices, and plantations in India, Malaysia, Indonesia, and Singapore.

ABC Natural Resources Pte Ltd (ABCNR) Singapore is one of Asia's fastest growing agro-focused conglomerates, with diverse interests in agro-commodity trading, the export and import of edible oils, and the cultivation of palm oil plantations. It has interests in value-added areas like oil mills, logistics, port facilities, and ocean carriers. The company's Singapore headquarters, ABCNR, is 100% subsidiary of ABC Oils Limited.

ABC Oils was a privately-held entity until 1990 when it became a public company. On February 8, 1993, the company became a publicly-listed company. The main objective of the company is manufacturing and dealing in oils, vegetable oils and fats, products from plantations, soaps, and allied products.

ABC Oils owns some of the big brands in the mustard oil segments. Brands held by the company include: Kalash Mustard oil, Double Sher Mustard oil, Crystal Clear (Soybean Oil), ABC Soya and ABC Gold refined oil, ABC Gold Vanaspati, ABC Gold plus Vanaspati.

The extracts obtained from the processing of mustard and soy seeds are formed into de-oiled cakes as by-products. Rich in proteins and micronutrients, these cakes have tremendous re-usable value as animal feed. Primarily used as cattle feed and farm input supplement, de-oiled cakes have a great demand across the world. ABC Oils exports most of its de-oiled cakes and this supplements the main business.

De-oiled mustard cake: the de-oiled mustard cake obtained from the extraction of mustard oil contains 1-2% of oil. This is used as a major ingredient of cattle feed in the country.

De-oiled soy meal: the husk that remains after the extraction of soybean flakes contains 50% soy protein and is used in the preparation of soy meal. This soy meal is rich in protein and is a natural energizer for livestock, poultry, and aquatic creatures.

Apart from generating the above by-products from the oil-extraction process, ABC Oils also helps in producing ABC bricks. The coal ash remnants from the plant's boilers are transported to the local brick kilns to be made into ABC bricks for the construction industry, boosting the local cottage industry of brick kilns.

To create optimum efficiency in the production process and reduce the use of natural resources, the waste water from cleaning the seeds is treated. This water is left with some remnants of oil in it. Using suitable separation processes, these compounds are recovered and transformed into products for use in agriculture and the environmentally-friendly bio-technology industry.

Additionally, ABC Oils have their own water treatment plant, which maintains a balance in the eco-system. The treated water is extensively recycled and used for farming and gardening in and around the factory.

ABC's consumer brands and products in mustard oil, soybean oil and palm oil are a household name with Indian consumers who use the oils regularly as a healthy cooking medium. A leader in mustard oil in India, ABC Oils today enjoys an 11% market share in the overall mustard oil segment, with a dominant 25% market leadership in branded mustard oil.

ABC Oils is an Indian company with an international footprint and global ambitions; a leader in the edible oil market in India, it generated a turnover of over Rs. 3,000 crores during the 2008-2009 financial year. Recently, the company has successfully undertaken the growth strategy of capacity expansion, green field projects and acquisitions, thus creating an unchallenged competitive advantage. With secured raw material supply sources, "near to customer" sales points and a robust distribution and dealer network, ABC Oils is creating market and brand leadership.

Over the past two decades, ABC Oils has built, nurtured and continually improved upon its various brands of edible oils. As a leading FMCG player in India and a leader in the mustard oil segment, ABC brands dominate the market, especially in east and north east India. Recently, the company has ventured into central and north India and the consumer response has been encouraging. Today, ABC brands are trusted by millions of consumers and are delighting their palates.

ABC brands comprise a range of healthy cooking oil brands in mustard, refined oil and vanaspati, thus catering to the tastes and preferences of different categories of consumers. The emphasis on "convenience" packaging of brands ensures that they meet the needs of consumers at every price point. All ABC brands have been developed on the basis of consumer feedback and preferences derived from in-depth market research. Over the years, the company has invested significantly in nurturing these brands in terms of quality, health, packaging and market penetration.

ABC has been able to create two very powerful brands in the mustard oil segment, which is a very significant achievement when one considers that 75% of mustard oil in India is sold loose. The company's strict adherence to quality, purity and delivering undiluted oil to consumers has won it unstinting loyalty from millions of homemakers who trust ABC Oils products as their cooking oil partner for the whole family. Each brand in the ABC basket has a distinctive positioning, catered to address a specific consumer need. The company invests significantly in creating brand awareness and consumer education, from TV commercials, to health camps, to promotions informing consumers of the health benefits of its products. It has created strong brand recall and loyalty in every Indian household.

The organization has as its mission the delivery of health and prosperity. ABC Oils is a leading Indian integrated edible oil company with a large base of ever-growing consumers. Over a period of two decades, the company has built a strong brand reputation and emotional connection with consumers for "delivering health and prosperity" through its consumer brands and products.

Its single-minded mission of "delivering health and prosperity" is driven by its belief that consumers need the best, pure, undiluted, edible oil as a cooking and health medium. This ensures that all the health properties of rich edible oils like mustard, palm and soybean are enjoyed and consumed by families. A healthy dietary pattern and intake of traditional oils like mustard oil helps maintain a healthy mind and body. ABC Oils' relentless focus on quality and hygiene has ensured that the "purity" and "freshness" of mustard and other oils are preserved until they reach the homes of the consumers in every part of the country.

ABC Oils will not do anything which does not result in "delivering health and prosperity". The mission is thus to ensure that, be it people, process and products, investors, vendors, partners or society as a whole, they will deliver the best value proposition as per global standards and international benchmarking, thus "delivering health and prosperity" in each and every field.

The company's mission of "delivering health and prosperity" helps to craft its future strategies for growth, thus creating better and new products for consumers and creating a value proposition which ensures that, through their actions, they deliver on promises to all stakeholders.

ABC Oils believes that growth has to be inclusive to become sustainable and that it is every business's moral responsibility to partner with society in its development. Stemming from this belief, it strives to shoulder its social responsibility in the best way and, today, in its own small way, contributes to the overall growth of the society around it.

Its initiatives have included setting up a school named Scholars' Public School and creating an eco-system of economic prosperity for the backward region of Morena. These are some of the initial steps in efforts to give back to the society in which ABC prospers.

ABC Oils is poised to become a true Indian MNC, with extended Indian presence and operations across the globe. It is a strong family of nearly 3000 employees spread over its six manufacturing plants, marketing offices, and plantations in India, Malaysia, Indonesia and Singapore. With the company registering explosive growth, the opportunities for fresh and experienced talent is immense both within Indian and overseas. A strong leadership team, comprised of the founders and senior industry professionals, have laid down a robust strategy with deliverable execution for the company, thus "delivering health and prosperity" not only to consumers but to every other stakeholder: employees, shareholders and investors, vendors, partners, and society as a whole.

As one of India's leading companies in the edible oil sector, ABC Oils has a deep understanding of agro-commodity and farmer community issues. Today, ABC Oils is part of the Indian growth story, using the country's inherent strength in agricultural resources and best managerial talent to serve millions of consumers in India and abroad. It is creating an Indian MNC with an international footprint of knowledge, leadership and value for its stakeholders across the globe. For many years, the performance of the company has been appreciable and it has been providing oil, vanaspati and other products with its well-furnished quality and purity.

Problem

The company was realising huge profits and had well-known market value according to market capitalization. The company clocked a turnover of Rs. 1030 crores during the first quarter of the 2010-2011 financial year. This was an increase of 13.56% from Rs. 907 crores during the corresponding period of the previous year. The company's net profit grew 2.64% to Rs. 50.51 crores for the quarter ending June 30, 2010, as compared to Rs. 49.21 crores during the corresponding period of the previous financial year.

But unfortunately, things did not remain the same, due to an income tax raid on K S Oils Limited on March 11, 2010, the financial position of the company started to rapidly decline. The income tax (IT) department raided premises owned by a leading edible oil manufacturer in over half a dozen cities in Madhya Pradesh and other parts of the country.

More than 250 IT staff, as well as staff from other departments, were engaged in raids on ABC Oils in Bhopal, Indore, Gwalior, Guna, Ratlam, Morena and Sheopur Kala, which began in the early morning. One of the BJP public statements stated that the highest income tax paid by Mr Garg had been Rs. 25 crores, and that's why he was raided.

After the IT raid, the share prices of the company started falling. This was because of the financial problems caused by the income tax raid. Additionally, Banmore and other organizations started denying funds to the company which resulted in it being unable to operate its manufacturing processes. No firm can run its business on its own money; all firms run on the basis of funds provided by shareholders and other sources.

These combined factors rendered the company incapable of paying its CC credit and it was not able to pay timely interest to the appropriate holders. Consequently, goodwill towards the company started to decline, not only in domestic but in foreign markets as well.

Since the holding company was facing all these problems, the subsidiary companies were also severely impacted. Gradually, the market news reached foreign markets from the domestic markets and the foreign investors greatly reduced their funding.

Finally, the wealth and value of the firm was not up to the mark in the domestic and foreign markets, according to market capitalization and turnover. The firm was not able to withstand these issues, hence the majority of the ABC Oils Ltd has now been sold out.

Questions:

1. Do a SWOT analysis of the company.
2. Critically analyse the case.
3. What went wrong?

6. Diva Life Insurance: A Case of Mis-selling

Diva Life Insurance Company Ltd is a joint venture company formed between Dabur, one of India's oldest and largest groups of companies, and Diva, the UK's largest and the fifth largest insurance company in the world. Dabur is India's leading producer of traditional healthcare products. Diva has a long history dating back to 1834. It was the largest foreign insurance provider in India during nationalization, in terms of the compensation paid by the Government of India. With respect to the regulations laid down by the Government of India, Diva has a 26% stake of the joint venture, while the Dabur group holds the remaining 74% of the stake.

Diva Life is backed by its strong skilled support staff. With its strong sales force of over 35,000 financial planning advisors, Diva has been able to initiate an innovative and differentiated sales approach to the business. Diva applies the ban assurance model in the country through its 40 ban assurance tie-ups. It also applies other forms of distribution networks to increase sales potential. Diva offers a wide array of life insurance products to cater to the needs of individuals and groups.

Through the concept of the "financial health check", Diva's sales force has established its credibility in the market. The "health check" is a free service provided in the societies administered by the FPAs to analyse the customer's long-term savings and insurance needs. Based on an analysis of the life and earning potential of the consumers, advisors can locate the right insurance product for each customer. Diva has an experienced team of fund managers and the options includes a unitized with-profits fund and seven unit-linked funds such as the protector fund, balanced fund, growth fund, enhancer fund and bond fund.

The Diva Money Back Plan is a traditional money-back plan with a bonus facility. In this plan, the premium needs to be paid until the end of the policy term or until death, if earlier. There is a guaranteed addition in the first three years and, after that, the policy participates in the simple reversionary bonus. Because this is a money-back plan, a certain sum of money is given back to the policyholder as survival benefit, as per the schedule mentioned at the time of the policy's inception. 120% of the sum assured + guaranteed additions – accrued bonus – all survival benefits already paid, is given to the policyholder at the end of the policy term as a maturity benefit. However, if the person whose life is insured dies within the policy tenure, the nominee would receive the entire sum assured as a death benefit, irrespective of the survival benefit already paid. This plan has guaranteed additions of Rs 40 per Rs 1000 sum assured, which is paid until the end of the policy term. This plan also has accidental death benefit as an additional rider.

Key Features of Diva Money Back Plan

- This is a traditional money-back plan with a bonus facility.
- Survival benefit is paid as per the schedule.
- This policy offers a guaranteed addition of Rs 40 per Rs 100 of the sum assured in the first three policy years.
- The policy participates in the bonus from the fourth policy year onwards.
- The full sum assured + guaranteed addition + accrued bonus are paid as a death benefit, irrespective of the survival benefit paid.
- 120% of the sum assured + guaranteed additions – accrued bonus – all survival benefits already paid is given to the policyholder at the end of the policy term as a maturity benefit.
- An accidental death benefit rider is available in this plan.
- This plan has a large sum assured rebate as well.

Eligibility of Diva Money Back

- Minimum entry age: 12 years old.
- Maximum entry age: 58 years old.
- Maximum age at maturity: 70 years old.
- Policy term: 12, 15, 18 or 21 years.
- Minimum premium: Rs 10,000 per annum.
- Minimum sum assured: Rs 1,00,000

Diva Money Back offer

Death Benefit:
In case the life assured passes away during the policy term, a sum assured with the relevant vested guaranteed additions and vested bonuses will be paid to the nominee.

Maturity Benefit:
A fixed percentage of the sum assured is paid on the due dates as per the policy term. On maturity, the guaranteed additions and sum assured are paid as well.

Guaranteed Addition:
These are made in the first three policy years.

Bonuses:
Reversionary bonuses are made from the fourth year onwards, along with a terminal bonus if any is added on maturity.

Riders:
An accidental death benefit rider can be adopted with the Diva Money Back plan.

Tax benefits:
- Under Section 80C, the customer can take a tax benefit. A yearly premium (of not more than 1lac) will be deducted from taxable income.
- Under Section 10(10D), a death claim is completely tax-free.

Details about the money-back plan:

Paid-up sum assured: After three policy years, if the customer is unable to continue the policy, they can convert to a pay-up policy. Moreover, the policy will not participate in future performance and, on maturity or death, a reduced sum assured with the guaranteed addition and any vested bonuses (if any) will be paid.

Surrender Value: In the event of cancelling the Diva Money Back plan after three years, the minimum guaranteed surrender value will be paid, which is equivalent to 30% of all premiums paid, barring the first year's premium.

Free Trial Period: The money-back plan can be cancelled within 15 days of receiving the policy contract. A written application can be submitted to any branch for the same. The premium will be paid back, minus some charges such as stamp duty, medical reports etc.

Case related to money-back policy

In 2008, one of the company's employees promised customers interested in a money-back plan that they would receive a bonus on their policy sum assured on the maturity date. Some customers accepted his proposal and took out a money-back plan. In this plan, for a customer to receive the money-back policy, they would have to pay a premium of 10,000 yearly on 1,00,000 and on the maturity date for 12 years. Previously, some consumers received the information that they would have to pay a premium total that was more than the sum assured of 1,00,000, providing a bonus on 1,00,000, but some policy holders should have received up to 1,20,000. The number of complaints grew and this resulted in the company having to make huge pay-outs, which caused huge losses. After this, the company changed its policy.

Questions:

1. Discuss the main issues involved in the case.
2. Give the probable solution to the case.

7. Working Capital Management at Gajraj Oils

The company was established in the year 1997 as a Kanchi Ghani mustard oil manufacturing unit. The unit made good progress and even surpassed its own estimates in every year of its operations. Initially, in 1998, the company established its unit at Galla Mandi, in the middle of Datia, in its own premises, but seeing the tremendous growth of the unit, management decided to shift the unit to a new location outside of the city. In 2001, the company opened a branch office at Etawah (UP) and another at Gwalior in 2003.

Previously, the company had been incorporated as a private limited company which turned into a limited company in 2004. Gajraj Oil and Foods Ltd (GOFL) were able to establish an impressive track record in the short period of eight years after its 1997 inception.

The company developed its brand, "DO PHOOL" and has created a positive image in the market in terms of quality and health safety. Now, "DO PHOOL" as a brand name is very famous in markets all across northern states like Madhya Pradesh, Uttar Pradesh, Chhatisgarh, Rajsthan, New Delhi, as well as north-east states like West Bengal, Assam and Bihar. Gajraj Group is ISO-9001 certified and is on its way to soon receive prestigious HACCP certification from the central government. The Group has also appointed dealers and distributors in different areas of the county and has a complete marketing network to promote its products.

The company owns 30 depots in various major cities and towns and has an extensive network of 500 dealers and 50,000 retailers in different parts of the country. It has established an impressive track record in terms of growth in sales, profitability, returns, market share, goodwill etc.

The company manufactures mustard oil (Sarson Tel) and wheat flour (Atta) and also processes sesame seed (Til) in its own state of the art manufacturing facilities located at Datia (65 km from Gwalior) and Malanpur Industrial Area (15 km from Gwalior).

Awards received

The company has received many awards and recognitions over the years which include:

> The Taste Awards: 2005 - Bronze
> The Taste Awards: 2005 - Silver
> The Taste Awards: 2005 - Gold
> The Taste Awards: 2006 - Gold

The Company's Financial Problem

When he reviewed the financial statements for 2009, the managing director of Gajraj Oil and Foods Ltd (GOFL) was surprised to find that there was a decrease in working capital for that year. He had planned to acquire a new machine by issuing shares and utilizing the year's profit. He had expected working capital to remain at the level of 2008.

The financial statements for the company are given below:

Balance Sheet as of March 31, 2009

	2009	2008
ASSETS	**Rs.**	**Rs.**
Current assets:		
Cash	5,25,000	7,50,000
Debtors	3,10,000	3,75,000
Stock	7,85,000	6,92,000
Prepaid expenses	15,000	18,000
Total current assets	16,35,000	18,35,000
Investments	4,00,000	2,80,000
Plant and machinery, Net of depreciation	18,00,000	8,00,000
Total assets	**38,35,000**	**29,15,000**
Liabilities		
Current liabilities:		
Creditors	2,10,000	2,29,000
Bank loans	1,20,000	1,12,000
Accrued expenses	50,000	36,000
Income tax payable	3,00,000	1,80,000
Total current liabilities	6,80,000	5,57,000
Debentures	7,50,000	9,00,000
Shareholder's equity:		
Share capital, Rs 10 par value	10,00,000	4,20,000
Share premium	4,00,000	2,80,000
Reserves and surplus	10,05,000	7,58,000
Total liabilities	**38,35,000**	**29,15,000**

Profit and Loss Account for the year ended March 31, 2009

	Rs.
Sales	34,00,000
Cost of goods sold (including machinery Rs. 1,40,000)	19,20,000
Gross profit	14,80,000
Operating expenses	7,80,000
Operating profit	7,00,000
Profit on sale of asset*	3,000
Profit before interest and tax	7,03,000
Interest	60,000
Profit before tax	6,43,000
Provision for tax	2,96,000
Net profit	**3,47,000**

* The book value of the equipment on March 31, 2008 was Rs. 4,000 and was bought for Rs. 10,000 six years ago. The equipment was sold at the beginning of April 2008.

Questions:

1. What do you understand by working capital management?
2. Analyse the case from financial point of view.

8. Max Targets at MAX!

MAX Bank Limited (formerly Melwyn Bank), is a financial services firm that began operations in 1994 after the Government of India allowed new private banks to be established. It is a public sector firm and its headquarters are located in Mumbai, Maharashtra (India). The key people of MAX Bank are Mr Adarsh Kishore, who is the chairman of the bank, and Mrs Shikha Sharma (managing director and chief executive officer). MAX Bank provides financial services and banking facilities. Its revenue is Rs. 19,826 crores, its net income is Rs. 3,344 crores, its total assets are Rs. 2,42,566 crores and its total number of employees is 21,640. The Bank was promoted jointly by the administrator of the specified undertaking of the Unit Trust of India (UTI-I), the Life Insurance Corporation of India (LIC), General Insurance Corporation Limited, the National Insurance Corporation Limited, the New India Assurance Company, the Oriental Insurance Corporation, and the United India Insurance Company. UTI-I holds a special position in the Indian capital market and has promoted many leading financial institutions in the country. The Bank changed its name to MAX Bank in April 2007 to avoid confusion with other unrelated entities with similar names.

In Gwalior, MAX Bank has two branches: one is at Kanwal Complex, Shrimant Madhav Rao Scindia Marg, City Centre, Gwalior; the other is at Huzrat Road, near Dewan Hospital, Lashkar Gwalior. Mr Rahul Sharma is working in MAX Bank's city centre branch as BDE (Business Developer Executive). In the face of slowing industry growth and new competition, today's retail banks are under tremendous pressure to grow organically. One of the core areas of business generation was selling different types of accounts to the customers, both individual and corporate. MAX offered different product ranges to the customers to meet their needs, in order to fight competition already present in the market.

The key challenges which the retail banking industry faced were increased competition and lower profit margins. Banks are dissatisfied with the results of their cross-selling/up-selling efforts and agent productivity continues to suffer. Achieving growth in retail banking is becoming increasingly difficult. Industry-wide, mortgage and deposit revenues are declining and credit card growth is stagnant. The ever-shrinking market share is split between more and more sources of competition.

In the last quarter (October to December) MAX Bank lost business totalling approximately Rs. 60 lakh from both of Gwalior's branches, because their sales of saving accounts, current accounts, salary accounts and life insurance went down by 66% in the last quarter (October to December). Banks responded to customer reluctance to engage in sales via remote channels by increasing investments in branches and by focusing branch activity on providing sales and advisory services.

With formidable competition from both traditional bricks and mortar operations and emerging banks, MAX was having trouble meeting performance expectations because they were unable to differentiate their business, reach customers likely to respond to new sales opportunities, or make the most of their valued staff.

Behind the Scenes

In the last quarter (October to December) MAX Bank lost business in the form of Rs. 60 lakh from both of Gwalior's branches because their sales of saving accounts, current accounts, salary accounts and life insurance went down by 66% in the last quarter. The reason behind this was that their six experienced BDEs left their jobs because in the previous six months they did not receive their incentives but were pressured for their sales to always be on top. BDEs had to open 20-22 accounts per month, but they could only open 8-12 accounts per month and the regional manager was not satisfied with those results.

Mr Rahul was not able to understand the precise nature of the problem. He was aware that initially, the commercialising of services through advertising mainly focused on extant services that people need. However, MAX has recently extended more persuasive messages through advertising, informing people about the goods and services that they should and ought to know about and buy for themselves. Selling these products and services through persuasive advertising messages is the result of advertising research. More specifically, consumer research tries to identify not only the socio-demographic, but also the psychographic profile of consumers, in order to understand how people can be persuaded to buy a company's product or service. Consumer research looks into the motivations and personalities of individuals in terms of consuming or buying a particular product or service, and then turns this information into strategies that are geared towards the company gaining a particular segment of the market. Even in full knowledge of this information though, a solution still was not known.

Questions:

1. Summarize the case.
2. What is the basic problem in the case?
3. Suggest some solutions to the case.

9. Delinquency of Demat Accounts at Rillan

The company was originally incorporated as "Rajeshwari Cosmetics Private Limited" on January 30, 1980. The name of the company was subsequently changed to "Rillan Enterprises Private Limited", pursuant to a special resolution of its shareholders dated January 10, 2006. The new certificate of incorporation, consequent to the change of name, was granted to the company on January 31, 2006, by the Registrar of Companies, Punjab, Himachal Pradesh and Chandigarh at Jalandhar.

The status of the company was changed to a public limited company by a special resolution of the members, and was dated July 14, 2006. The new certificate of incorporation consequent upon the change of name was granted to the company on August 11, 2006 by the Registrar of Companies, NCT at New Delhi. At the time of incorporation, the main objective of the company was to purchase, sell, import, export, manufacture, pack, replace or otherwise deal in all types of toothpaste, toothbrushes, face powder, face cream and other cosmetics.

Rillan is a Pharma P promoted group

The Indian pharmaceutical industry is centre stage in the global healthcare arena, and Pharma P endeavours to be at the forefront by delivering India-centric advantages to the advanced and developing countries of the world. From a small domestic company at inception, Pharma P has grown formidably to be the billion-dollar institution that was envisioned by the late Dr Raghuvinder Singh, who was the chairman and managing director of Pharma in the early 1990s.

Rillan Securities Limited

RSL is one of the leading brokering houses of India. It deals with equity broking, depository services, portfolio management services, institutional equity brokerage and research, investment banking and corporate finance. Rillan is a Pharma P promoter group company and is one of India's largest and fastest growing integrated financial services institutions. The company offers a large and diverse suite of services ranging from equities, commodities, and insurance broking, to services such as wealth advisory, portfolio management, personal finance, investment banking, and institutional broking. The services are broadly clubbed across three key business verticals: retail; wealth management; and the institutional spectrum. Rillan Enterprises Limited is the holding company for all of its businesses, structured and being operated through various subsidiaries. It has a huge network over the length and breadth of India with more than 1837* locations across more than 498* cities and towns. Just select a place and you'll find a manager to assist you there. Having spread itself fairly well in the world and promising not to rest on its laurels, it has also aggressively started eyeing global geography. Extending its services has been a constant feature of Rillan's attention to the needs of their clients. Consequently, the company has launched internet trading and merchant banking, to take care of the different investment needs of different classes of investors. To facilitate free and fair trading processes, Rillan is a member of major financial institutions like the National Stock Exchange of India and the Bombay Stock Exchange of India, and is a depository participant with the National Securities Depository Limited and Central Depository Services (I) Limited. It is also a SEBI-approved portfolio management service, which is a platform from which all segments of investors can take advantage of the opportunities offered by investing in Indian equities, either on their own or through managed funds in portfolio management.

Rillan's team is led by a very eminent board of directors, which provides policy guidance and work under the active leadership of its CEO and managing director, and the support of its central guidance team.

Products and Services of Rillan Securities Ltd

Rillan is one of the heavyweight equity players in India with membership of the National Stock Exchange of India and the Bombay Stock Exchange – both major exchanges of India. It believes in innovative services that could cater to a range of customers according to their requirements. Rillan equity and derivative trading is offered in two unique ways:

Demat: In India, the term "demat" refers to a dematerialized account for individual Indian citizens to trade in listed stocks or debentures in electronic form, rather than paper, as required for investors by the Securities and Exchange Board of India (SEBI). In a demat account, shares and securities are held electronically instead of the investor taking physical possession of certificates. A demat account is opened by the investor while registering with an investment broker (or sub-broker). The demat account number is quoted for all transactions to enable electronic settlements of trades to take place.

Access to the demat account requires an internet password and a transaction password. Transfers or purchases of securities can then be initiated. Purchases and sales of securities on the demat account are automatically made once transactions are confirmed and completed.

The Indian Market

The capital market in India has seen an unprecedented boom in the last 15 years, in terms of number of stock exchanges, listed companies, trade volumes, market intermediaries, and the investor population. However, this surge in activity created many initial problems, due to the large volumes of paperwork. Large volumes of trading, clearing and settlements using only paper-based instruments were beset with problems that threatened the very survival of India's capital market.

Until the late 1980s, the common man kept away from capital markets and, therefore, the amount of funds mobilized through the market was relatively meagre. Indian markets were overwhelmed by paper shares, which were becoming increasingly tedious to maintain. Problems such as fake and stolen shares; fake signatures and signature mismatches; the duplication or mutilation of shares; and transfer problems plagued the traditional paper-based trading and settlement system. On top of all these risks, the system had cumbersome procedures and excessive paperwork that deterred both retail and institutional investors from entering the capital market. Investors felt under-compensated for the risks borne by them. Thus, the lack of modernization in a large, inefficient system became a major hindrance to the growth of the capital market.

Real growth and improvement appeared in the early nineties in the wake of the economic liberalization initiatives of the Indian government. Economic reforms were envisaged in various financial sectors: banking, capital markets, securities, market regulation, mutual funds, foreign investments and government control. Financial institutions and stock exchanges knew that stock certificates were the main cause of investor disputes and arbitration cases. The traditional paper-based system simply could not keep up with the rapid pace of economic growth, and an advanced alternative was mandated.

The Government of India decided to set up a fully-automated exchange model that could offer screen-based trading and depositories, to eliminate various bottlenecks in the capital market, particularly in the clearing and settlement system in stock exchanges.

- Trading in securities may become uncontrolled in the case of dematerialized securities.
- It is incumbent upon the capital market regulator to keep a close watch on the trading in dematerialized securities and see to it that trading does not act as a detriment to investors.
- For dematerialized securities, the role of key market players (such as stockbrokers) needs to be supervised as they have the capability to manipulate the market.
- Multiple regulatory frameworks have to be conformed to, including the Depositories Act, regulations and by-laws of various depositories.
- Agreements are entered into at various levels of the process of dematerialization. These may cause anxiety to the investor who desires simplicity.

Problem

Rillan Gwalior's branch manager, who had been there since its inception, was facing trouble. The sales people were able to sell the demat account and the targets were also met. But the issue was different. The customers who were interested in the securities or dealing in any other commodities were opening their demat accounts with very small amounts. The accounts were opened up with just marginal amounts of money. Another issue related to this was that even after opening the account, the trading was not done through that account, which was being opened just for its name. As the accounts were open accounts (though no trading was done), the company had to maintain all of them. The people, time, and money of the organization were all engaged in this. The company expected to earn profits through the operation of these accounts but they were not generating any kind of revenue. So, it was actually more expenditure for the company, rather than profit being earned. Also, the business needs were different as markets are highly volatile and competitive and there are higher risks, such as client default, high leverage offered to customers, higher operational costs, human resource costs, infrastructure costs, and lower profit margins. These add to the expenditure of the organization. On several occasions, the branch manager was asked to provide an explanation for costs being incurred in such a way, but he was helpless: if he hadn't sold the accounts, targets would not have been met; by selling the accounts, operational costs increased. He was in dilemma about what to do and what not to do!

Questions:

1. What do you understand by demat accounts? Why are they beneficial?
2. What is the problem faced by the company?
3. What you would have done if you were in the branch manager's place?

10. EVA Implementation:
The Case of Pavitra Group

This case is based on the case study of Godrej India, published by Icrmindia.

PCPL is part of the Pavitra Group, which is one of the largest engineering and consumer products companies in the country. It has varied interests, from engineering to personal care products, with a total sales turnover of about 1100 million USD. As one of India's outstanding industrial corporations, Pavitra has become a household name for several generations of Indians. The Pavitra Group was established in 1887 and has since grown into a billion-dollar conglomerate. The parent company's commitment is truly reflected in its mission of "enriching value of years each day all over", and with its vision: "Pavitra in every home and work place". The company is based on the four pillars of integrity, service, trust and respect. The Pavitra label has come to mean different things to different people, the length and breadth of India. Companies operating under the group umbrella are involved in a wide range of businesses, from locks and safes to typewriters and word processors, from refrigerators and furniture to machine tools and process equipment, from engineering workstations to cosmetics and detergents, from edible oils and chemicals to agro products. One such part of the Pavitra Group is Pavitra Consumer Products Ltd (PCPL).

The CPG segment ranks among the the best implementers of information technology. Some of the prominent areas where CPG organizations are harnessing the power of IT include supply chain management, dealer management, customer relationship management and sales force management. CPG companies are also one of the highest spenders on information technology.

Pavitra Consumer Products Limited: economic value added (EVA); deployment of EVA framework; maximizing shareholders' wealth; EVA in the FMCG industry; FMCG industry in India; calculation of EVA; capital asset pricing model; approaches to calculate capital employed; Scorpio; commercial vehicles; innovations in the road transportation industry.

Introduction

The term "economic value added (EVA)" is a registered trademark of Stern Stewart and Co. of New York City (USA). In his book, *The Quest for Value* (1991), Bennett Stewart used the term EVA with a symbol ™ as super script, which is normal practice when referring to any registered trademark whenever the term is used. EVA is therefore actually Stern Stewart and Co.'s trademark for a specific method of calculating economic profit. Peter Drucker claimed that he discussed EVA in his 1964 book, *Managing for Results*. However, it cannot be denied (without going into an argument about who invented EVA first) that the concept only became popular after Stern Stewart and Co. marketed it.

Using different metrics in order to evaluate the performance of a company is considered a rather complex procedure, but one of crucial importance for any economic organization. It might reveal unidentified problems which, if settled, would improve the general position of the firm and boost it in the future. Economic value added (EVA) is an alternative to the traditional accounting profits; it has fanatic advocates as well as opponents. The real value created for a firm has great significance for shareholders, since they often feel unprotected against the bad decisions and choices made by the managers. A system like EVA, which motivates managers to think and act like shareholders and rewards them accordingly, is presented by the advocates of EVA as the key to answering such a question. This study examines this problem based on a case study approach.

EVA focuses attention on how a firm uses its capital by asking, "Is a firm generating earnings above and beyond that expected by the market (the providers of the capital)?"

Stern: "Some may say that EVA was a fad of the 1990s, but earning more than the cost of capital is not a fad. It is what all companies should do all of the time. That they do not is surprising. All of the talk on governance, also not a fad, never demanded this simple requirement. Until boards do, EVA will remain as relevant as it was in the 1990s."

The relevant formula is:

EVA= (Return on Capital - Cost of Capital) x Total Capital

We need three figures:

1. **NOPAT**
2. **Investment**
3. **WACC**

By dividing NOPAT with investment, we get returns in percentage. From this, we deduct AWCC, which is also in a percentage. The difference would show %profit per rupee. By multiplying this with total capital, we capture EVA in rupee-terms.

Moving Further

Basant Pavitra, the chairman of the Pavitra Group, publicly announced on July 29, 2001, that the Group had successfully implemented the economic value added (EVA) framework. It took ten months for Stern Stewart and Co., the originator of EVA, to implement it in the Pavitra Group.

Although EVA was globally a very widely accepted framework, it was a new concept in India. Very few companies like TCS and NIIT had adopted EVA in the country by mid-2001. While the Pavitra Group adopted EVA, industry analysts were busy debating the pros and cons of it in general, and for the Group in particular. A few weeks after the EVA announcement, Basant declared the half yearly financial results of Pavitra Consumer Products Limited (PCPL) for the quarter period that ended September 30, 2001. The revenues had grown by 19% to Rs 2.529 bn, as against the growth of 15% in the corresponding period in 2000. PCPL reported an EVA of Rs. 0.137 bn for the six months that ended September 30, 2001. Announcing the results, Basant said, "Our strong focus on EVA has delivered rising profitability".

EVA was considered a complex concept in India at that time. Some analysts raised doubts as to whether Basant would be able to efficiently use EVA to increase shareholders' value in the future. Reportedly, Basant's ability was being questioned because many joint ventures and alliances had previously failed. Allaying all doubts, Basant said, "'I met up with the CEOs of both TCS and NIIT, and they advised not to complicate the exercise in the beginning."[4] He indicated that the concept would be simplified for easy implementation in the company. However, financial analysts were not satisfied with Basant's statement. They commented that EVA was not an efficient financial tool to deliver improved profitability within a short time period. In their opinion, EVA was an accounting measure that could be easily manipulated by accounting tricks. Analysts felt that Basant had adopted the EVA framework only to achieve a better market valuation of the consumer product division of the Group, represented by PCPL.

Why EVA?

There are two very good reasons why EVA is much better than ROI (RONA, ROCE, ROIC) as a controlling tool and as a performance measure.

1. Steering failure in ROI
Increase in ROI is not necessarily good for shareholders, i.e. maximizing ROI cannot be set as a target. (An increase in ROI would be unambiguously good only in companies where capital can be neither increased nor decreased -> however we live in a world where both operations are easily executed in almost all companies)

2. EVA is a more practical and understandable approach than ROI as an absolute and income statement-based measure. EVA is quite easily explained to non-financial employees. Furthermore, the impact of different day-to-day actions can be easily turned into EVA-figures, since an additional $100 cost decreases EVA by $100. ROI is neither easy to explain to employees nor can day-to-day actions easily be expressed in terms of ROI. This particular benefit of EVA is often totally forgotten in academic discussion since it cannot, of course, be seen in desk studies or empirical studies which try to trace the correlation between EVA and share prices.

Apart from globally renowned products, they had the financial and technical muscle to dominate the Indian FMCG market. The problem was further exacerbated when the joint venture (JV) of PSL with Procter and Gamble (P and G) came to an end in 1996. Recalling the bad phase, Press said, "It hadn't been always so rosy for Pavitra. There was a time when the company was struggling to keep pace with the changes of liberalization and the challenges of competition." PSL faced problems on several fronts, including HR and marketing. After the dissolution of the JV, many capable managers left the company. Moreover, PSL was not able to attract new talent because most of them preferred working in MNCs.

The Main Reason

Some analysts argued that PSL's move to adopt EVA was a well-considered plan. PSL had two divisions: PCPL and PIL. The PCPL division was responsible for managing the consumer products business, while PIL managed the chemicals and food business. Analysts opined that the product portfolio of PSL had become very large and unrelated, ranging from soaps to detergents to food and chemicals. The growth in the product segments was not same. For instance, the consumer products business was performing better than the chemicals and food business (see Table II). PSL hired KoMak, a financial advisory services company in India, to decide the fate of the PIL division, which was affecting PSL's financial performance.

The Consequences: One month before the demerger, the shares of PSL were trading at Rs 85 on the Bombay Stock Exchange (BSE). Soon after the demerger, both the companies witnessed distinct financial and stock market performances.

On July 18, 2001, PCPL was listed on the Bombay Stock Exchange quoted at Rs 58.50, while PIL traded at Rs 18. By August 2002, the share price of PCPL rose to Rs. 120, while that of PIL remained stagnant at Rs. 20. Analysts said that this vast difference in share prices showed investors' perceived value of the two companies. PCPL was outperforming PIL, not only on the stock exchanges but also by reporting better financial performance. With the significant rise in PCPL's share prices, the shareholders of the company were delighted. As PSL was a closely held company, the biggest shareholders were the promoters themselves.

How Effective was EVA?

EVA, an income measure, was calculated by subtracting the cost of capital from the post-tax operating profit (NOPAT) generated by a company. EVA measured whether the post-tax operating profit of a company was enough to cover its cost of capital. Unlike the traditional methods of accounting profit, where only the cost of debt was deducted, EVA also took into account the cost of equity. Therefore, EVA tried to capture the true economic profit of an enterprise. EVA was more directly linked to the creation of shareholder wealth over time. It could be calculated as net operating profit minus an appropriate charge for the opportunity cost of all capital invested in an enterprise.

Conclusion

The EVA-based performance measurement system is the basis upon which a company should take appropriate decisions related to its choice of strategy, capital allocation, mergers and acquisitions, divesting business and goal setting. While deciding resource allocation it becomes necessary to appreciate the EVA impact on such decisions. Management accountants have full knowledge of what would create value in a company and are in the position to guide it through a restructuring mission for value-creation. So, a management accountant is expected to successfully transform a traditional management system into a value-based management system. The present case discusses the implementation of the economic value added (EVA) framework in Pavitra Consumer Products Limited (PCPL), a traditional FMCG company in India. It covers, in detail, the reasons for implementing the EVA framework in PCPL and the benefits derived by the company from it. The case then examines the nexus between the implementation of the EVA framework and improvement in the financial performance of the company. It ends with a debate about the effectiveness of EVA and highlights its limitations.

Questions:

1. Summarize the case.
2. Do a SWOT analysis of the company.
3. Why is EVA better than other performance measures?
4. Would you suggest that an organization takes steps to achieve EVA implementation?

11. A Case Related to Mishra Ltd and MDBI Bank

It was a troublesome morning for the Mishras. They were scratching their heads, attempting to come to a conclusion, and blaming one of the well-established banks in the Indian market, MDBI Bank. The Mishras had been jointly issued with a pre-sanction letter in the names of both the brothers, Mr Ravi Mishra and Rohan Mishra, from MDBI Bank. On the basis of the pre-sanction letter being issued to the Mishras jointly, it included the home loan pertaining to the property they had finalized at Harishankarpuram, sector-3.

The pre-sanction letter provided approval for the amount of 50 lacs, a loan based upon consideration of the financial strength of both brothers, on submission of the required documents. The property deal was finalized at 48 lacs, i.e. within the approval limit being sanctioned to them.

When they approached the bank to issue the sanction letter and subsequent disbursement of the loan amount, they were surprised to discover from bank officials that, in normal circumstances, the MDBI Bank does not disburse home loans to two brothers in joint names. The Mishras were taken aback by this response, which caused them to engage in a verbal altercation with the bank's officials. Their main point of contention was that the bank officials had "issued a pre-sanction jointly in the name of both the brothers". To that end, an enquiry was carried out into whether it was communicated to them that the loan could not be disbursed jointly in both of their names. Of course, the brothers' contention is that they would have approached other banks if they had been made aware of the bank's stance.

The Mishras visited MDBI Bank on a later date where they met with Mr Vikas, the head of the branch, and provided him with the pre-sanction letter with which they had earlier been issued. Mr Vikas discussed the issue with his colleague and finally assured them that they would seek approval from their boss, Mr Srinivas, and would communicate his response to them in two days. Mr Vikas also conceded that it was the bank's mistake to issue the pre-sanction letter in joint names.

The grievance was further exacerbated when Mr Vikas informed the Mishras that they would have to submit LIC policies to the tune of Rs. 5 lacs as additional collateral security, since the loan was in the joint names of both brothers. Although they were not informed about this at the time of seeking pre-sanction approval, they nonetheless extended their full co-operation to the bank and provided them with the LIC policies of Mr Ravi and Rohan Mishra to the extent of Rs. 2.5 lacs each.

Nevertheless, the issues did not abate. Rather, the Mishras were then told that that they would need to provide the bank with the surrender value of the policies. However, as the policies had not yet been issued for three years, the Mishras did not yet have their surrender value. Again, the Mishras were assured by Mr Vikas that he would try to address their problem with higher authorities, to waive the three-year period for subsequent approvals.

In short, although the Mishras had wholeheartedly extended their co-operation to the bank to expedite the process of disbursement of a home loan, they did not receive the sanction letter and had to forgo the property deal, resulting in them suffering a huge financial loss; their future investment and other activities depended a lot on their ability to close the deal and, the owner of the property was not willing to co-operate with them.

Questions:

1. Summarize the case.
2. What are the documents required for the sanctioning of a loan?
3. Critically analyse the case and give solutions from your perspective.
4. What should organizations do to prevent such problems occurring?

12. Financial Performance: The Case of Saraswati Auto Industries

Saraswati Auto Industries Limited is one of the most renowned companies in the world. They are pioneers in manufacturing load springs in India. Their product is branded as "SAI Springs".

SAI Group was started in 1955 by the visionary, Sardar Jupinder Singh Jauhar, chairman and managing director. The chief unit is in Yamuna Nagar. Under the able guidance of Sardar Jupinder Singh, the company grew to become the fourth largest leaf spring manufacturer in Asia. SAI is certified by TS16949 and the company is now managed by the two dynamic sons, Mr R.S. Jauhar, who is the C.E.O of the company, and P.S. Jauhar, who is the C.O.O of the SAI Group.

The group has two plants, one at Malanpur (near Gwalior) in the Bhind District of Madhya Pradesh, and the other at Yamuna Nagar, in the state of Haryana. Both plants are effectively managed by a team of qualified professionals. The Malanpur plant started operations in 1963, when it started production of leaf springs and it has the distinction of being India's first leaf spring plant. This is the only company to have the manufacturing facilities for parabolic springs. The other plant at Yamuna Nagar is ISO 9002 certified.

Financial Performance

SAI Ltd has an audit committee which is responsible for the effective supervision of the financial and accounting controls, as well as compliance with the financial policies of the company. The committee interacts with the auditors to ascertain the quality and precision of the company's transactions, to review the manner in which they are performing their responsibilities, and to discuss the reports of the auditors.

The sources of funding of SAI Ltd are both internal and external. Internal sources of funds include collections against sales. External sources of funds include loans from banks or financial institutions, and these are of two types:

(1) Team loan
(2) Working capital loan

A team loan is used for machinery, usually for purchase and maintenance. A working capital loan is obtained for running the plant. Again, these are of two types:

(a) Fund based
(b) Non-fund based

Fund-based Activities:

- Underwriting of or investment in shares, debentures, bonds, etc. of new issues;
- Dealing in secondary market activities (for buying and selling);
- Participating in money market instruments such as commercial papers, certificates of deposits, treasury bills, discounting of bills, etc.;
- Involvement in equipment leasing, hire purchase, venture capital, seed capital, etc.

Non Fund-based Activities:

These are otherwise known as fee-based activities, and include:
- Managing the capital issues;
- Making arrangements for the placement of capital and debt instruments with investment institutions;
- Arrangement of funds from financial institutions for the client project cost, or the working capital requirements.

Non fund-based working capital loans consist of a letter of credit and a bank guarantee.

SAI Ltd uses all types of books, including cash book, bank book, journal, ledger, etc. for accounting purposes.

As SAI manufactures springs, the various payments that have to be made include:

a) Raw material payments
b) Manufacturing expenses payments
c) Salary and wages
d) Administrative expenses
e) Selling expenses

f) Bank
g) Repayment of loan

Balance Sheet - Saraswati Auto Industries Ltd in Rs. Cr.

	Mar 11	Mar-10	Mar-09	Mar-08	Mar-07
	12 mths	12 mths	12 mths	12 mths	12 mths
EQUITIES AND LIABILITIES					
SHAREHOLDER'S FUNDS					
Total Share Capital	42.78	40.04	40.03	37.37	17.71
Reserves and Surplus	91.58	34.92	27.13	33.15	-2.61
Total Shareholders Funds	134.35	74.95	67.16	70.52	15.11
NON-CURRENT LIABILITIES					
Long Term Borrowings	49.1	108.8	141.9	131.09	73.29
Total Non-Current Liabilities	59.07	137.52	166.61	155.46	86.73
CURRENT LIABILITIES					
Total Current Liabilities	298.39	182.49	143.85	156.6	75.65
Total Capital And Liabilities	491.82	394.96	377.62	382.58	177.48
ASSETS					
NON-CURRENT ASSETS					
Fixed Assets	192.68	162.54	152.53	132.61	63.64
Total Non-Current Assets	262.19	235.9	223.73	193.17	96.88
CURRENT ASSETS					
Total Current Assets	229.64	159.06	153.9	189.41	80.6
Total Assets	491.82	394.96	377.62	382.58	177.48

Financial Crises

The 2008-2009 period was, in many ways, a landmark year, not only for the company but also globally. The year began on a very optimistic note for the company with a first quarter (April-June 2008) turnover of Rs. 184.92 crores, and all economic indicators indicating robust GDP growth of 9-10% for 2008-09.

The Indian economy, stock market and practically all business forecasts painted a very bright business environment. The first quarter performance was an all-time high and had raised high expectations of a record turnover and profit. Seeing the April 2008 production and sales trend, the company had geared itself up to achieve a record turnover of Rs. 780 crores for 2008-2009 and was expecting a good jump in its profits.

Work was also in full swing in the Jamshedpur plant, to expand capacity. However, these expectations were met with a rude awakening when a few US banking giants collapsed, resulting in massive losses suffered by major international banks in USA and Europe. India did not remain immune from the global financial crisis and there were strong signs of a slowdown from September 2008 onwards.

These events were so sudden that no one was prepared for such a rapid decline in economic cycles the world over. The signs of slowdown were also visible for the business: from the second quarter (July-Sept 2008), sales went down to Rs. 158.51 crores. The situation became worse in the third quarter (October-December 2008) as the company's sales sharply went down to Rs. 78.42 crores. The February and March demand provided a glimmer of hope and revival and, in the fourth quarter, sales rose to Rs. 110.48 crores.

Cumulative sales for the year 2008-09 were Rs. 513.78 crores and the net loss was Rs. 16.39 crores. Production of commercial vehicles (CVs) and multi-utility vehicles (MUVs) declined by 35% in 2008-2009 at 637,000 vehicles.

The sudden and unprecedented decline in production and sales from mid-September 2008 until January 2009 adversely impacted the company's financial performance. As a result, "the management had taken a number of steps to combat the slowdown". These included improving the productivity of manpower, machines and available resources; cutting wastage and costs; and detecting and plugging all revenue leakages. All the capital expenditures were kept on hold. The company decided to increase its share in the domestic and export replacement markets.

The organization was happy to report that it was able to increase its share in the domestic replacement market. The month of February 2009 brought some cheer as there were signs of a pick-up in demand, which provided hopes of a revival in the economy and the company's fortunes. The company ended the year with gross sales of Rs. 513.78 crores, as against Rs. 541.19 crores in 2007-08. Net loss for 2008-09 was Rs. 16.39 crores, as against net profit of Rs. 16.06 crores in 2007-08. Production trends for the current year are now available and all indicators suggest an increase in demand.

Questions:

1   Summarize the case.
2. What do you understand by financial crisis? What were the reasons for crisis in the case?
3. Critically analyse the financial performance of the organization.
4. Suggest some measures to improve the financial performance of the organization.

13. Mis-selling: The Case of Parv Money Life Insurance

Parv Money Life Insurance Company Limited and Parv Money General Insurance Company Limited (collectively "Parv Money") are joint ventures of the Parv Group and the American International Group, Inc. (Money). Parv Money combines the strength and integrity of the Parv Group with Money's international expertise and financial strength. The Parv Group holds a 74% stake in the insurance venture, while Money holds the balance at 26%. Parv Money Life provides insurance solutions to individuals and corporate clients. Parv Money Life Insurance Company was licensed to operate in India on February 12, 2001 and started operations on April 1, 2001. It won the Company of the Year Award 2011 in the health insurance category and the Best Product Innovation Award 2011 in the general insurance category

Case

A channel partner, Saroj Khan, sold one of Parv Money's policies to a customer called Ganesh. The details of the policy were as follows: the name of policy was Big Life Gold; the maturity period was 100 years; and the premium paying term was 15 years (traditional plan). The channel partner sold the policy by stating that if the customer purchased this plan, the money would double in five years if the customer deposited the amount of RS 1,00000 within one year.

It transpired that the customer was not eligible to take out that policy because of their age. In addition, the plan was traditional in nature, which dictated that the premium had to be paid for 15 years without lapsing. If the customer failed to pay any premium, then the amount would be converted into a non-interest bearing amount, because the company would not provide any return or interest.

When the company sent a reminder to the customer, he contacted the channel to ascertain the reason for the call. It was at that time that he came to discover that the channel partner of Parv Money had mis-sold the plan. The customer complained about this to the operation channel (Parv Money) and this complaint was forwarded to the legal department. After a long investigation, the department discovered that there was no mistake made by the customer and that the real culprit was the channel partner.

On account of this fact, the company paid Rs 70000 to the customer, which represented a financial loss for the company and a future loss of Rs 900000.

Questions:

- What do you understand by insurance?
- What are different types of insurance?
- What is misselling?
- Critically analyse the case.
- Discuss the role of IRDA in insurance regulation.

14. RK Industries: A Case Study on Estimation of Working Capital

RK Tyre commenced operations in 1977 when it set up its first tyre manufacturing plant, with an installed capacity of 500,000 tyres per annum, in Kankroli, Rajasthan. In order to keep pace with the growth in the market and the demand for its products, RK Tyre established a new state-of-the-art passenger radial manufacturing facility at Banmore, near Gwalior in Madhya Pradesh. In 1997 it made a strategic acquisition of Vikrant Tyre, a Government of Karnatak undertaking. In a short period of time, RK Tyre had turned it into a quality, driven company with all four accreditations (ISO 9001, QS 9000, ISO 14001 and TS 16949). This indeed is a true reflection of RK Tyre's commitment to systems and its quality-oriented approach.

The tyre industry in India is estimated at Rs. 22,500 crores (US$ 4.70 billion) and has a direct co-relation with the automotive industry, economic growth, infrastructure development and the road transportation sector. Over the last five years and to keep pace with economic growth, the Indian tyre industry has consistently notched up a compounded annual growth rate (CAGR) of 8%. This ride, however, hit a speed breaker in 2008 with the economic slowdown and increased input costs. Tyre industry growth, registered at an impressive 10.40% in 2007/08, declined to 2.40% in 2008/09. However, with the recovery in the economy, it was estimated that the Indian tyre industry would register growth between 5% and 6% in 2010 and further gain momentum in subsequent years. Five tyre majors control nearly 80% of the Indian tyre industry. The truck and bus segments contribute almost 75% to its rupee value turnover. With India emerging as a global automotive hub, domestic tyre companies are expanding their operations and global tyre majors are increasing their presence in the Indian tyre market. The new technological frontiers of the tyre industry in India are radicalisation in the truck and bus segments and a shift to high-performance tubeless passenger car radials. As a pioneer in radial technology in India, RK Tyre has now unleashed yet another radial revolution in the truck and bus segments and has grown consistently faster than the industry. Today, the company is poised to capture a substantial part of future growth. This is partly being made possible by expanding capacity at its existing plants, and partly by establishing new production facilities.

Product

Riding on more than three decades of technological innovation and breakthroughs, RK Tyre today offers a wide range of 4-wheeler tyres for virtually every requirement – heavy commercial vehicles (HCV), light commercial vehicles (LCV), passenger vehicles, tractors and off-the-road (OTR) tyres. The company markets its entire product range under its flagship brand, RK Tyre. The company's brand portfolio also includes Vikrant and Tornel. In the truck bias segment, which accounts for 75% of its revenue, RK Tyre has created various power brands like Jet Trak, Jet Xtra, Jet R Miles, Jet Rib, and Jet Trak 39, all of which are segment leaders and are renowned for their performance. To harness both technology and innovation, the company has founded the Hari Shankar Singhania Elastomer and Tyre Research Institute (HASETRI), which is among Asia's foremost research and development centres. Independent of this, RK Tyre has also established the Raghupati Singhania Centre of Excellence, in a joint venture with IIT Chennai, for advanced studies into vehicle dynamics. These R&D facilities enable the company to bring world-class products to the Indian market and help it to partner with automotive manufacturers, right from the drawing board.

Promotion

RK Tyre has always innovatively engaged and bonded with its customers through a sustained presence in mass media with relevant advertising. Its recent campaign "Made for India and Made for You" is built around the advantages of using RK truck and bus radial tyres. At the same time, the company has been actively promoting its range of premium tubeless car radials, Vectra and Ultima NXT. The company realises that consumers will best benefit from modern technology only when they are fully informed and completely empowered. RK Tyre reaches out to vehicle owners through extensive ground connect campaigns. The primary focus is to impart knowledge about tyre care and usage so that consumers can derive optimum performance from their tyres and gain from that experience. The company is now focusing on leveraging contemporary and innovative media tools for higher consumer connection and interaction. Each year, the company has been conducting a unique nationwide tyre care initiative branded "Cool Wheels". Over several years, RK Tyre has leveraged its status as a premier tyre manufacturer by energetically associating with various national and international motor sports events. Participating in motor sports helps the company to continuously update its products to meet the challenges posed by gruelling conditions. The company has built a complete infrastructure for motorsports in India and, in the last eleven years, invested over Rs. 70 crores (US$ 14.60 million) in developing it. The RK Tyre National Racing and Karting Programme is a nursery for the country's motorsport talent. Several of today's prominent names such as Narain Karthikeyan, Armaan Ebrahim, Karun Chandhok, Ashwin Sundar and Aditya Patel, amongst other emerging names, have all been products of this facility. These efforts have laid the foundations for India to join the F1 circuit. Always conscious of its responsibilities towards the communities in which it operates, RK Tyre has taken concrete steps to realise its social commitments. Over the years, the company has supported numerous environmental and healthcare programmes and several social, cultural and educational initiatives.

Working Capital

Working capital (WC) is a financial metric which represents the operating liquidity available to a business, organization, or other entity, including government entity. Along with fixed assets such as plant and equipment, working capital is considered part of the operating capital. Net working capital is calculated as current assets minus current liabilities. It is a derivation of working capital that is commonly used in valuation techniques such as discounted cash flows (DCFs). If current assets are less than current liabilities, an entity has a working capital deficiency, also called a working capital deficit.

Net Working Capital = Current Assets − Current Liabilities
Net Operating Working Capital = Current Assets − Non Interest-bearing Current Liabilities
Equity Working Capital = Current Assets − Current Liabilities − Long-term Debt

A company can be endowed with assets and profitability but be short of liquidity if its assets cannot readily be converted into cash. Positive working capital is required to ensure that a firm is able to continue its operations and has sufficient funds to satisfy both maturing short-term debt and upcoming operational expenses. The management of working capital involves managing inventories, accounts receivable and payable, and cash.

Current assets and current liabilities include three accounts which are of special importance. These accounts represent the areas of the business where managers have the most direct impact:

- Accounts receivable (current assets)
- Inventory (current assets)
- Accounts payable (current liability)

The current portion of debt (payable within 12 months) is critical, because it represents a short-term claim to current assets and is often secured by long-term assets. Common types of short-term debt are bank loans and lines of credit.

An increase in working capital indicates that the business has either increased its current assets (that is, it has increased its receivables or other current assets) or has decreased its current liabilities (for example, by paying off some short-term creditors).

Implications for M&A: The common commercial definition of working capital for the purposes of a working capital adjustment in an M&A transaction (i.e., for a working capital adjustment mechanism in a sale and purchase agreement) is equal to:

Current Assets – current liabilities excluding deferred tax assets/liabilities, excess cash, surplus assets and/or deposit balances. Cash balance items often attract a one-for-one purchase price adjustment.

Decisions relating to working capital and short-term financing are referred to as working capital management. These involve managing the relationship between a firm's short-term assets and its short-term liabilities. The goal of working capital management is to ensure that the firm is able to continue its operations and that it has sufficient cash flow to satisfy both maturing short-term debt and upcoming operational expenses.

Decision Criteria

By definition, working capital management entails short-term decisions generally relating to the next one-year period, which is "reversible". These decisions are therefore not taken on the same basis as capital investment decisions (NPV or related, as above), but rather, they will be based on cash flows and/or profitability.

One measure of cash flow is provided by the cash conversion cycle, the net number of days from the outlay of cash for raw material to receiving payment from the customer. As a management tool, this metric makes explicit the correlation between decisions relating to inventories, accounts receivable and payable, and cash. Because this number effectively corresponds to the time that the firm's cash is tied up in operations and unavailable for other activities, management generally aims at a low net count.

In this context, the most useful measure of profitability is return on capital (ROC). The result is shown as a percentage, determined by dividing relevant income for the 12 months by the capital employed. Return on equity (ROE) shows this result for the firm's shareholders. Firm value is enhanced when, and if, a return on capital (which results from working capital management) exceeds the cost of capital, which results from capital investment decisions, as above. ROC measures are therefore useful as a management tool, in that they link short-term policy with long-term decision-making. See economic value added (EVA).

Credit policy of the firm: Another factor affecting working capital management is the credit policy of the firm. It includes the buying of raw material and selling of finished goods, either in cash or on credit. This, in turn, affects the cash conversion cycle.

Management of working capital

Guided by the above criteria, management will use a combination of policies and techniques for the management of working capital. These policies aim at managing the current assets (generally cash and cash equivalents, inventories and debtors) and the short-term financing, such that cash flows and returns are acceptable.

Cash management: Identifies the cash balance which allows the business to meet day-to-day expenses, but reduces cash holding costs.

Inventory management: Identifies the level of inventory which allows for uninterrupted production but reduces the investment in raw materials – and minimizes reordering costs – and hence increases cash flow. Besides this, the lead times in production should be lowered to reduce work in progress (WIP) and, similarly, the finished goods should be kept on as low a level as possible to avoid over-production (see supply chain management; just in time (JIT); economic order quantity (EOQ); economic quantity).

Debtor's management: Identifying the appropriate credit policy, i.e. credit terms which will attract customers, such that any impact on cash flow and the cash conversion cycle will be offset by increased revenue. Based on the above discussion, details are shown below for the best method-selection for WC calculations.

Three methods of calculating optimum working capital requirement

Method 1: current asset holding period
Assumptions
Inventory: One month's supply of each raw material, semi-finished goods, finished goods.
Debtors: One month's sales.
Operating Cash: One month's total cost.
Rs. In Cr.

ITEM \ YEAR	2011	2010	2009	2007	2006
RAW MATERIAL	320.93	194.21	193.11	167.75	161.82
SEMI-FINISHED	339.92	211.68	208.15	180.93	174.09
FINISHED	393.356	260.043	248.850	221.926	211.304
TOTAL INVENTORY	1054	665.993	650.11	570.60	547.223
DEBTORS	590499	40.633	24.581	36.293	39.824
OPERATING CASH	393.356	260.043	248.850	221.926	211.304
TOTAL WORKING CAPITAL	1507.06	966.60	923.541	828.825	798.351

The first method gives details of the working capital items. This approach is subject to error if the market is seasonal.

Method 2: ratio of sales
Assumption: 30% of annual sales

ITEM \ YEAR	2011	2010	2009	2007	2006
TOTAL WORKING CAPITAL	1574.271	1186.887	1098.063	958.713	885.807

The second method has limited reliability. Its accuracy is dependent upon the accuracy of sales estimates.

Method 3: ratio of fixed investment
Assumption: 20% of fixed investment

ITEM / YEAR	2011	2010	2009	2007	2006
TOTAL WORKING CAPITAL	283.262	270.554	220.2	239.76	244.838

Third method relates working capital to investment. If the estimate of investment is accurate, this method cannot be relied upon.

Conclusion

We can now conclude that a number of factors govern the choice of method for estimating working capital. Factors such as seasonal variation in operation, accuracy of sale forecast, investment cost, and variability in sale price would generally be considered. The production cycle and collection policy of the firm would have an impact on working capital requirement.

Questions:

1 What do you understand by working capital management?
2. Discuss the various aspects discussed in the case.
3. Summarize the case.

15. JRF Ltd. Case: Inaccurate Sales Forecasting

In relation to a wide range of products, JRF is not only the largest manufacturer of technical textiles in India but also enjoys global leadership in most of the products under the umbrella of its business. As well as India, it has manufacturing plants for technical textiles in the United Arab Emirates (UAE), Thailand and South Africa. Equipped with state-of-the-art R&D facilities, JRF's largest business also enjoys an enviable reputation for possessing unmatched technical competency and credibility in the market. JRF's product basket for technical textiles contains nylon tyre cord fabrics, polyester tyre cord fabrics, belting fabrics, coated fabrics, laminated fabrics, fishnet twines and industrial yarns. The technical textiles are high-performance fabrics that are mainly used for non-consumer applications. JRF Ltd began operating in 1974 with the manufacture of nylon tyre cord fabric. Today, it is a clear domestic market leader in its three core businesses of technical textiles, chemicals and packaging films.

In 2005-2006 it posted profits of Rs.104.77 crores, on net sales of Rs.1297.56 crores. Its nearly 2200 employees operate out of its 14 locations in India, UAE and USA, which include four plants (three in India and one in Dubai). Already the seventh largest manufacturer of nylon tyre cord fabric in the world, and the fifth largest manufacturer of belting fabrics, JRF aims to be among the top three global players in each of its businesses over the next five years.

In 2011, JRF adopted the tight inventory control system because of a shortage of financial resources. The company therefore produced and stocked goods according to the tight sales forecasts. This was implemented because they were running short of financial resources, forcing them to adopt the tight inventory control system despite the liberal one which they generally adopted. Because of the policy changes, they started maintaining inventories below their target level, but it was observed that the policy of tight inventory control resulted in substantial sales losses. It was noticed that the company started losing orders because of stock outages.

The problem of lost sales forced the management to reconsider its inventory policy. They therefore reconsidered the whole matter again with the help of a committee, consisting of experts of finance, marketing and production to determine whether the level of the finished goods inventory should be increased. After their investigation into the case they observed (on more than the stiffness of the current inventory control system), the problem was found to be based on inaccurate sales forecasts. Because of the inaccurate sales forecasts, the entire problem was created, although a tight inventory control system also, to some extent, contributed to the problem. Although the committee found that wrong forecasts were the problem, the inventory management system couldn't be left without comment, and the company is still looking for a solution.

Questions:

1. What is to be understood by inventory management? What are the different ways of inventory control?
2. What kind of inventory management policy was followed by JRF India? What were the reasons for this?
3. What is sales forecasting?
4. Find out the problem in the case and give a suitable solution to the case.

16. Financial Fury of Mehta India

Mehta India Limited is a company which was incorporated in Calcutta. The company manufactures and markets all types of footwear, footwear components, leather and products allied to the footwear trade. Mehta was originally promoted as Mehta Shoe Co. Pvt Ltd, by Leader AG, Switzerland, a member of the Toronto-based multinational, Mehta Shoe Organisation (MSO). It became a public limited company in 1983 and the name was changed to Mehta India Ltd. In 1952, in addition to the footwear manufacturing plant, a machinery department was set up which produced the first Indian-made major shoe machine. A leather footwear factory was established at Patna, Bihar, which today is known as Mehtaganj. In 1973, it came up with the public issue of capital in June, when Leader AG, Switzerland, offered 5,00,000 shares for sale out of their holdings at a premium of Rs 20 per share (2,00,000 shares each to LIC and UTI, and 1,00,000 shares to the public).

Leader AG, Switzerland, offered for sale 8,00,000 shares at a premium of Rs 8/- per share to resident Indian nationals, thereby reducing their holdings to 12,00,000 shares or 40% of the issue capital in 1977. Another 47,14,000 equity shares, at Rs 10 each, at a premium of Rs 25 per share, were issued to Mehta (BN) B.V., Amsterdam, a wholly owned subsidiary of Leader AG, Switzerland, in order to raise their holding in the company from 40% to 51%.

Case of Mehta India HR Problem

More than half of Mehta's production came from the Mehtanagar factory in Bengal, a state notorious for its militant trade unions deriving their strength from the dominant political parties, especially the parties on the left. Notwithstanding the giant conglomerate's grip on the shoe market in India, Mehta's equally large reputation for internal corruption created the perception that Weston would have a difficult time. When the new management team weeded out irregularities and turned the company around within a couple of years, tackling the politicized trade unions proved to be the hardest of all tasks.

While he was attending a business meeting at the company's factory at Mehtanagar on July 22, 1988, Weston was severely assaulted by four workers. The incident occurred after a member of BMU, Arup Batra, met Weston to discuss the issue of the suspended employees. Batra reportedly got into a verbal duel with Weston, upon which the other workers began to shout. When Weston tried to leave the room, the workers turned violent and assaulted him. This was the second attack on an officer since Weston had taken charge of the company, the first one being the assault on the chief welfare officer in 1986.

For the right and wrong reasons, Mehta India Limited (Mehta) always made the headlines in the financial newspapers and business magazines during the late 1990s. The company was headed by the 65 year-old managing director, John Keith Weston (Weston). He was popularly known as a "turn specialist" and had successfully turned around many ailing companies within the Mehta Shoe Organization (MSO) group. By the end of financial year 1999, Mehta managed to report rising profits for four consecutive years, after incurring its first ever loss of Rs 420 million in 1995. However, by the third quarter, which ended on September 30, 2000, Weston was a worried man.

Mehta was once again on the downward path. The company's nine month's net profits of Rs 105.5 million in 2000 was substantially lower than the Rs 209.8 million recorded in 1999. Its staff costs of Rs 1.29 million (23% of net sales) was also higher, compared to Rs 1.18 million incurred in the previous year. In September 2000, Mehta was heading towards a major labour dispute as the Mehta Mazdoor Union (BMU) had requested that the West Bengal government intervene in what it considered to be a major downsizing exercise.

Background Note: With revenues of Rs. 7.27 billion and net profit of Rs. 304.6 million for the financial year ending December 31, 1991, Mehta was India's largest manufacturer and marketer of footwear products. As on February 08, 2001, the company had a market valuation of Rs. 3.7 billion.

For years, Mehta's reasonably priced, sturdy footwear had made it one of India's best known brands. Mehta sold over 60 million pairs per annum in India and also exported its products to overseas markets including the US, the UK, Europe and the Middle East. The company was an important operation for its Toronto-based parent, the BSO group, run by Thomas Mehta, which owned a 51% equity stake.

The company provided employment to over 15,000 people in its manufacturing and sales operations throughout India. With the headquarters based in Calcutta, the company manufactured over 33 million pairs per year across its five plants located in Mehtanagar (West Bengal), Faridabad (Haryana), Bangalore (Karnataka), Patna (Bihar) and Hosur (Tamil Nadu). It had a distribution network of over 1,500 retail stores and 27 wholesale depots. It outsourced over 23 million pairs per year to various small-scale manufacturers.

Mehta India Balance sheet (2006-2010) in Rs. Cr.

	Dec '10	Dec '09	Dec '08	Dec '07	Dec '06
	12 months	12 months	12 months	12 months	12 months
Sources of Funds					
Total Share Capital	64.26	64.26	64.26	64.26	64.26
Equity Share Capital	64.26	64.26	64.26	64.26	64.26
Share Application Money	0	0	0	0	0
Preference Share Capital	0	0	0	0	0
Reserves	299.3	233.84	189.17	147.23	119.22
Revaluation Reserves	34.68	36.18	37.72	39.89	28.52
Net worth	**398.24**	**334.28**	**291.15**	**251.38**	**212**
Secured Loans	0	14.65	35.91	45.07	48.06
Unsecured Loans	13.77	10.4	8.72	6.73	0.27
Total Debt	**13.77**	**25.05**	**44.63**	**51.8**	**48.33**
Total Liabilities	**412.01**	**359.33**	**335.78**	**303.18**	**260.33**
Application of Funds					
Gross Block	417.56	374.4	349.34	324.52	306.58
Less: Accum. Depreciation	264.44	244.12	232.31	220.6	227.17
Net Block	**153.12**	**130.28**	**117.03**	**103.92**	**79.41**
Capital Work in Progress	0.32	0.63	0.86	0.31	0.84
Investments	**17.25**	**17.25**	**17.25**	**17.25**	**17.24**
Inventories	299.36	277.46	292.23	303.74	276.36
Sundry Debtors	30.2	25.18	25.89	22.86	21.61
Cash and Bank Balance	15.65	17.44	8.8	13.81	4.16
Total Current Assets	345.21	320.08	326.92	340.41	302.13
Loans and Advances	175.27	107.33	96.75	53.24	43.43
Fixed Deposits	119.92	38.77	17.96	18.91	10.14
Total CA, Loans and Advances	640.4	466.18	441.63	412.56	355.7

Deferred Credit	0	0	0	0	0
Current Liabilities	313.14	193.28	194.36	198.4	177.71
Provisions	85.94	63.26	54.26	33.65	15.17
Total CL and Provisions	399.08	256.54	248.62	232.05	192.88
Net Current Assets	**241.32**	**209.64**	**193.01**	**180.51**	**162.82**
Miscellaneous Expenses	0	1.53	7.65	1.2	0
Total Assets	**412.01**	**359.33**	**335.8**	**303.19**	**260.31**
Contingent Liabilities	72.53	50.83	54.62	82.07	127.35
Book Value (Rs)	56.57	46.39	39.44	32.91	28.55

Questions:

1. Summarize the case
2. What is the problem in the case?
3. Analyse the financial aspects of the company using the details given.

17. Avoidable Payment of Interest on Income Tax

> **The company made an avoidable payment of 1.96 crore towards interest/penalty due to a delayed submission of income tax returns and non-remittance of advance income tax.**

Under sections 208, read with sections 209, 210 and 211 of the Income Tax Act (1961), it was mandatory for the company to pay advance income tax (AIT) in four quarterly instalments during each financial year (on or before 15 June, 15 September, 15 December and 15 March), in case the amount of income tax payable was 5,000 or more. Further, according to sections 234 (A), (B) and (C), if the assesse does not submit an income tax return (IT return) on the due date, or fails to pay AIT, the assesse is liable to pay simple interest at the rate of one percent per month, for every month of belated/non-submission of the IT return, and for a shortfall or belated remittance of quarterly AIT.

It was observed that the company, with a view to taking advantage of the tax exemption on the taxable income applied (March 2008), registered as a charitable institution under section 12A of the Income Tax Act (1961). The income tax authorities accordingly fixed the date for hearing the case as September 15, 2008, and instructed the company to provide necessary details/records in support of their claim.

The company, however, failed to appear before the tax authorities on the date fixed and present its case for claiming the tax exemption. The claim of the company was, therefore, rejected (September 18, 2008) by the income tax authorities.

It was observed that although the company applied for tax exemption under section 12A of the Income Tax Act (1961) in March 2008, it had not deposited AIT since its incorporation in July 2004 (financial years 2004-05 to 2007-08) on the assumption that the company would be granted tax exemption by the tax authorities. The company also failed to submit IT returns for these years within the time limit prescribed under section 139 (1) of the Act. The non-payment of AIT and belated submission of returns attracted interest payments under sections 234 (A), (B) and (C) of the Act. As a result, the company had to pay interest of 1.96 crore, which could have been avoided by timely payment of the quarterly instalments of AIT, and by filing IT returns on due dates, as per the provisions of the Act.

While admitting the stated facts in February 2010, that the company submitted an application to register the organization under section 12A of the Income Tax Act (1961) to claim income tax exemption, when it was rejected by the commissioner for income tax, the company preferred an appeal rather than an income tax tribunal. As a result, the company had to pay the tax along with the interest. The government endorsed the response of the management.

The plea of the company was not valid because the company did not apply for tax exemption under section 12A of the Income Tax Act (1961) until March 2008, but failed to submit an income tax return in time and had not deposited AIT since its incorporation in 2004-05, which is not justified.

Questions:

1. Critically analyse the problem in the case.
2. Summarize the case and give its solution.

18. A Case Study on Working Capital Loans at IMFC Bank

The India Money Finance Corporation Limited (IMFC) was amongst the first to receive an "in principle" approval from the Reserve Bank of India (RBI), to set up a bank in the private sector, as part of the RBI's liberalization of India.

Background

The India Money Finance Corporation Limited (IMFC) was amongst the first to receive an "in principle" approval from the Reserve Bank of India (RBI) to set up a bank in the private sector, as part of the RBI's liberalization of the Indian banking industry in 1994. The bank was incorporated in August 1994 under the name of "IMFC Bank Limited", with its registered office in Mumbai, India. It commenced operations as a scheduled commercial bank in January 1995.

Business Focus

IMFC Bank's mission is to be a world class Indian bank. The objective is to build sound customer franchises across distinct businesses. The aim of this is to be the preferred provider of banking services for targeted retail and wholesale customer segments, and to achieve healthy growth in profitability, consistent with the bank's risk appetite. The bank is committed to maintaining the highest levels of ethical standards, professional integrity, corporate governance and regulatory compliance. IMFC Bank's business philosophy is based on four core values: operational excellence; customer focus; product leadership; and people.

Capital Structure

As of June 30, 2010, the authorized share capital of the bank is Rs. 550 Cr. and the paid-up capital is Rs. 459, 69, 07,030/- (45, 96, 90,703 equity shares of Rs. 10/- each). The IMFC Group holds 23.63% of the bank's equity. About 17.05% of the equity is held by ADS Depository (in respect of the bank's American depository shares (ADS) issue). Foreign Institutional Investors (FIIs) hold about 27.45% of the equity, and the bank has about 433,078 shareholders.

The shares are listed on the Bombay Stock Exchange Limited and the National Stock Exchange of India Limited. The bank's American depository shares (ADS) are listed on the New York Stock Exchange (NYSE) under the symbol "HDB". The bank's global depository receipts (GDRs) are listed on the Luxembourg Stock Exchange under ISIN No US40415F2002.

Distribution Network

IMFC Bank has its headquarters in Mumbai. As of March 31, 2011, it had a distribution network of 1,986 branches, spread across 996 cities in India. All branches are linked on an online real-time basis. Customers in over 500 locations are also serviced through telephone banking. The bank's expansion plans take into account the need to have a presence in all major industrial and commercial centres where corporate customers are located, as well as the need to build a strong retail customer base for both deposits and loan products. Being a clearing/settlement bank for various leading stock exchange companies, the bank has branches in the centres where the NSE/BSE has a strong and active member base. It also has 5,471 networked automated teller machines (ATMs) across these cities. Moreover, IMFC Bank's ATM network can be accessed by all domestic and international Visa/MasterCard, Visa Electron/Maestro, Plus/Cirrus and American Express credit/charge cardholders.

Management

Mr C.M. Vasudev was appointed as chairman of the bank, with effect from July 6, 2010, subject to approval by the Reserve Bank of India and the shareholders. Mr Vasudev has been a director of the bank since October 2006. A retired IAS officer, he has had an illustrious career in the civil service and has held several key positions in India and overseas, including Finance Secretary for the Government of India, Executive Director of the World Bank, and a government nominee on the boards of many companies in the financial sector.

The managing director, Mr Aditya Puri, has been a professional banker for over 25 years. Before joining IMFC Bank in 1994, he headed Citibank's operations in Malaysia. The bank's board of directors is composed of eminent individuals who have a wealth of experience in public policy, administration, industry and commercial banking.

Technology

IMFC Bank operates in a highly automated environment in terms of information technology and communication systems. All the bank's branches have online connectivity, which enables it to offer speedy funds transfer facilities to its customers. Multi-branch access is also provided to retail customers through the branch network and automated teller machines (ATMs).

IMFC Bank has made substantial efforts and investments in acquiring the best technology internationally available, to build the infrastructure of a world class bank. Its business is supported by scalable and robust systems which ensure that its clients always get the finest services that they offer. The bank has prioritized its engagement in technology and the internet as one of its key goals and has already made significant progress in web-enabling its core enterprises in each of its businesses.

How to Manage a Working Capital Loan

Working capital loan funds provide a business with the cash it needs to keep growing until it can cover all operating expenses out of revenue. Without a working capital loan, most businesses become unable to generate enough revenue to stay afloat. These funds provide access to cash which can be used to pay rent or mortgage payments, utilities, marketing expenses, inventory, employees, etc. Obtaining capital through this method can be difficult for many businesses, so it is essential to have good business credit scores.

Establishing and building solid business credit scores is key in obtaining substantial working capital loan funds that can be used to grow a business. Not all types of working capital require business credit history, but it is important to have that in place. Lenders use business credit scores just like they use personal credit scores when evaluating whether a business is worthy of receiving capital. Ensuring that lines of credit help to build credit, puts you in the right position, to get the loans that your business needs to succeed.

There are five common types of working capital loan:

Equity: This is obtained from personal resources like equity in your house, funds from friends or family members, or from angel investors etc.

Trade Creditor: A trade creditor will extend a loan to you so you can purchase a large quantity from their place of business. They will often check your business credit history before extending credit to you.

Factoring /Advances: You can sell future credit card receipts for instant capital if your business accepts credit cards. Another option is to sell your accounts receivable to a factoring company who handles the collection.

Line of Credit: Your business can apply for a bank line of credit, giving you the ability to borrow for short-term needs. Good business credit scores will assist with your approval for a line of credit.

Short term loan: A bank can also extend credit to allow you to purchase inventory for a season. This note will typically be less than a year. Again, good established business credit scores will almost guarantee access to this kind of funding

Analysis of the Schedule in Change in Working Capital

The below table provides a detailed analysis of the schedule in change in working capital for IMFC Bank, for the years 2010 and 2011.

Particulars	Year 2010	Year 2011	Effect on W.C	
			Increase	Decrease
CURRENT ASSETS				
Inventories	312181368	249232511	-	62948857
Sundry Debtors	176256 876	166547181	-	9709695
Cash and Bank	1231881	1176728	-	55153
Loan and Advances	53602290	52926780	-	639510
Total Assets(A)	**543272415**	**469919200**		
CURRENT LIABILITIES				
Acceptances	1437839	1064519	373320	-
Due to small scale Industries	13330138	31946661	-	18616523
Other creditors	474508263	351553825	122954483	-
Security Deposit	161577377	191870540	-	30293163
Advance Receipt from customer	6087877	7771805	-	1683928
Provision for gratuity	106843171	116083324	-	9240153
Total of Current Liabilities (B)	**763784665**	**700290674**		
W.C. (A-B)	(220512250)	(230371474)		

Neg. decreases in W.C.	9859224		9859224	
Total	(230371474)	(230371474)	133186982	133186982

Problems:

The above schedule of the change in working capital has different problems:

1. What is the reason for increasing current liability and provision by 1.5 Cr.?
2. Why did the debtors decrease by 0.97 Cr.?
3. How did the cash and bank balance decrease?
4. Why did the inventory decrease by 6 Cr?

The main objective is to identify the problem faced by banks, regarding working capital loans.

19. A Case Study on Samachar Rozana Problems Related to E.O.Q.

Introduction

With a readership of 1.84 crore, the brand ROZANA is today synonymous with success, quality, change, dynamism, and ethics in millions of households across India and the corporate world alike.

From the humble beginnings of one Hindi edition from Jabalpur in 1968, today the group has grown to become India's largest newspaper group. It has a strong presence in newspapers, radio, event marketing, printing, short code, and internet portal. With its flagship Hindi daily newspapers, SAMACHAR ROZANA; Gujarati Daily; Divya ROZANA; the Marathi daily, Divya Marathi; and the English daily, DSR, it covers 15 states with 84 editions. In addition to these, it also publishes Business ROZANA, DB Star and magazines like Aha! Zindagi, Bal ROZANA, Young ROZANA and Lakshay. The other media businesses include MY BIG radio (radio channel), 545667 (Short Code), and IMCL (internet services).

History

The SAMACHAR ROZANA group is a multifaceted industry major, founded half-a-century ago. The group's initial enterprise was in the newspaper publication business. Over the years, the group has diversified into sectors such as textiles, solvent extraction, oil refinery, vanaspati, exporting polished/semi-precious stones, TV media, FM radio, information technology, real estate, theme/amusement parks, and FMCG. Indeed, under the stewardship of Shri Suresh Chandra Agarwal, the group has taken an honourable place among India's corporate elites.

Product Dealings

Media business
- Newspapers: SAMACHAR ROZANA, Divya ROZANA, DSR, SR Star, Business ROZANA, Subah Kiran, and Divya yotiRadio – MY BIG radio
- Digital Media: ITCL, IISL
- Magazines
- SR Activation

- DTV

Non-Media Businesses

- Power Sector
- Solvent Extraction
- Textiles: Denims
- Hotel
- Infrastructure
- FMCG

Social Initiatives

- ROZANA Foundation
- Taj 7 Wonders
- Water Conservation
- Kid Valley School
- Abhidharshan

In 1996, the 40 year-old Bhopal-based newspaper group had a circulation of 350,000 copies per day in Uttar Pradesh. By 2004, this had grown by more than 1000% to 3.5 million (2.3 million in Hindi and 1.2 million in Gujarati) across six states in India: Madhya Pradesh, Chhattisgarh, Rajasthan, Haryana, Chandigarh and Gujarat, making it one of the top 25 dailies in the world. In a little over ten years, ROZANA achieved circulation figures that others in the global newspaper business had taken nearly a century to achieve. Today, ROZANA has a collective circulation of approximately 4.4 million across its titles, SAMACHAR ROZANA, Divya ROZANA, Saurashtra Nav Samchar, Subah Kiran, Business ROZANA, SR Star and DSR.

ROZANA's rapid growth has occurred in an unlikely setting. All the large, powerful media groups in India operate in the English language. Although Hindi is the most widely used spoken language in India, the vernacular press is highly segmented with small, regional papers holdings sway. No local language newspaper has been able to cut across states the way English newspapers have. Further, the newspaper business was, and still is, a game of slow growth over generations of readers. People don't easily change newspaper-reading habits and, if they do, it takes several years of persistent wooing to get them to shift.

But consider this. In Jaipur (its first city of launch outside Madhya Pradesh), SAMACHAR ROZANA entered the market as number one, with 172,000 copies on December 19, 1996. In its next new market, Chandigarh, it was again number one, with 69,000 copies when it launched in May 2000. In its third launch - the state of Haryana - it entered as number one with 271,000 copies in June 2000. And in its fourth launch, in Ahmedabad on June 23, 2003, it entered as number one with 452,000 copies, a world record. It expanded into Gujarat in a matter of fifteen months, entering the two other major cities of Gujarat: Surat and Baroda. It currently has nine editions in Gujarat and is the largest circulated Gujarati daily, with 11.5 Lakh copies according to the Bureau of Circulation. It continued this in Punjab in 2006, launching simultaneously from Amritsar and Jallandhar with 178,000 copies. These are results that make one sit up and say "Wow"!

The usual question is how did the SAMACHAR ROZANA group increase circulation by a factor of ten in such a short time and in such a hostile environment? The larger questions are: What did these guys do differently from the others in the newspaper industry? What is replicable in what they did? What can organizations in other industries learn from them?

To understand the nature of ROZANA's achievement, one has to understand industry dynamics. Every industry is made up of a leader and followers. The leader is there by virtue of some outstanding strategy or because they started the industry. The followers try to emulate the leader but, since the latter has enormous advantages of efficiencies and market share, the former never quite catches up, although he is kept on his toes. This pattern persists across industries and this state of affairs continues for years.

MEETING THE CHALLENGE HEAD-ON: When ROZANA began with the aspiration of entering Jaipur as number two with a print run of 50,000 copies, it demolished all the industry entry and growth barriers. Every industry paradigm would necessarily have to be reconsidered. Every industry has its entry barriers and its growth barriers. In addition, everyone in the industry operates within them. The entry barriers keep newcomers out and the growth barriers maintain the status quo. If you are number one or two that's a very comfortable situation but, sooner or later, along comes a bright-eyed orbit shifter who refuses to play by the rules, and suddenly all the barriers that you thought had foundations in concrete tumble like a house of cards. The group therefore decided to go in for a truly in-depth understanding of the readership patterns in the city. Unlike a conventional survey that takes a random sample size and tries to extrapolate information into a broad need or trend, the SAMACHAR ROZANA group decided to meet a whopping 200,000 potential newspaper-buying households in Jaipur!

SAMACHAR ROZANA group launched Nav Marathi's second edition from Nasik on July 3, 2011. This is the second edition of the Marathi language newspaper, following its launch in Aurangabad. An issue they had to deal with was how much to produce, because the paper used for manufacturing newspaper can be purchased in bulk and used in the future. However, the problem was the use of ink, as the same ink cannot be used for long because it can dry up. Therefore, according to new technology, the KBA machine should be used for printing.

Printing Technology

The KBA machine.

The mammoth 8-storey high printing configuration, manufactured by Koenig and Bauer AG of Germany, has fully computerized systems to control vital functions: colour registration; ink water balance; speed; cut-off; conveying printed copy to the stacker where the copies are counted as per the labels; labelling; poly-film wrapping; and strapping into complete bundles ready for dispatch. This is all completed without any manual intervention. It prints 85,000 copies per hour, against the normal average yield of 30,000 copies per hour. The machine enhances the reading and visual experience by:

- Producing shaper and crisper images due to metal back blankets.
- Producing sharper and brighter text.
- Being very near to the original colour visual reproduction.

This technology has reduced printing time from 45 minutes to 11 minutes. It facilitates on-time deliveries of newspaper to depots packed with automated machines, with the precise numbers of copies, thereby eliminating shortages and damaged copies. All supplements are pre-inserted which eliminates manual insertion by hawkers, saving considerable time and effort on their part. That means a saving of time at both the printing and delivery end of newspaper, which enables the newspaper to go to print later than usual. This results in even late news hitting the stands.

The machine allows many innovations like flap printing, pop-ups, drop outs, double-width central spread etc. In the high technology machine, the ink is also manufactured by Koenig and Bauer AG of Germany, hence confusion can arise in ordering quantity.

SAMACHAR ROZANA has received an offer of quantity discounts on its order of material, by Koenig and Bauer AG of Germany

Ordering Quantities (in litres)	price per quantity (per litre)
Less than 5000	12
5000 but less than 16,000	11.80
16,000 but less than 40,000	11.60
40,000 but less than 80,000	11.40
80,000 and above	11.20

The annual requirement for the material is 80,000 litres. The ordering cost per order is Rs.12.00 and the stock holding is estimated at 20% of material cost per annum. What should EOQ be?

20. SMT Ltd.: A Case Study on Working Capital Management

With a wide range of products, SMT is not only the largest manufacturer of technical textiles in India but it also enjoys a global leadership for most of the products within this business. Apart from India, its manufacturing plants for technical textiles are present in the United Arab Emirates, Thailand, and South Africa. Equipped with state-of-the-art R&D facilities, SMT's largest business also enjoys an enviable reputation of possessing unmatched technical competency and credibility in the market. SMT's product basket for technical textiles contains nylon tyre cord fabrics, polyester tyre cord fabrics, belting fabrics, coated fabrics, laminated fabrics, fishnet twines, and industrial yarns. The technical textiles are high-performance fabrics that are mainly used for non-consumer applications. SMT Ltd, which commenced operations in 1974 with the manufacture of nylon tyre cord fabric, is today a clear domestic market leader in its three core businesses of technical textiles, chemicals, and packaging films. SMT began as Shri Ram Fibres in 1970, when its parent company, DCM, decided to set up a separate entity to manufacture nylon tyre cord fibres. Its formation was a result of the foresight that nylon was the future material for tyre cord fibres.

The company established its first plant in Manali, near Chennai, in 1973. With an initial annual capacity of 2000 tonnes of nylon cords, the plant started operations in 1974. Shri Ram Fibres thus became one of the first companies in India to start manufacturing nylon tyre cords. Over the years, the company expanded its product line in technical textiles and also diversified into other businesses like chemicals, packaging films, and engineering plastics. The company was no longer manufacturing fibres alone, a fact that necessitated the change in its name. Shri Ram Fibres thus became SMT in 1990.

In 2005-2006, it posted profits of Rs.104.77 crores on net sales of Rs.1297.56 crores. Its nearly 2200 employees operate out of its 14 locations in India, UAE and USA. This includes four plants: three in India and one in Dubai. Already the seventh largest manufacturer of nylon tyre cord fabric in the world, and the fifth largest manufacturer of belting fabrics, SMT aims to be among the top three global players in each of its businesses over the next five years.

The Case of Working Capital Problem at SMT Ltd

Overtrading

Overtrading takes place when a business accepts work and tries to complete it, but finds that fulfilment requires greater resources (more people, working capital or net assets) than are available. This is often caused by unforeseen events, such as when manufacture or delivery take longer than anticipated, and can result in cash flow being impaired. Overtrading leads to cash flow problems, most often because of a lack of working capital. A typical scenario is that cash inflows from sales (especially sales on credit) come in too late to pay suppliers for the increase in stocks required. Another common scenario (in construction for example) is that wages may have to be paid, and equipment and material obtained, long before a customer pays for the completed work.

Large amount of assets

Working capital is a measurement of an entity's current assets, after subtracting its liabilities. Sometimes referred to as operating capital, it is a valuation of the amount of liquidity a business or organization has for the running and building of the business. Generally speaking, companies with higher amounts of working capital are better positioned for success. They have the liquid assets needed to expand their business operations as desired.

Sometimes, a company will have a large amount of assets, but have very little with which to build the business and improve processes. Even a profitable company may have this problem. This can occur when a company has assets that are not easy to convert into cash.

Working capital can be expressed as a positive or negative number. When a company has more debts than current assets, it has negative working capital. When current assets outweigh debts, a company has positive working capital.

Changes in working capital will impact a business's cash flow. When working capital increases, the effect on cash flow is negative. This is often caused by the liquidation of inventory or the drawing of money from accounts that are due to be paid by the business. On the other hand, a decrease in working capital translates into less money to settle short-term debts.

Solution to overtrading:
➢ Businesses can avoid overtrading through good planning (so that they can ensure that resources are available when required, before problems occur), and by being well-financed (so, for example, funds are available to increase working capital if required).
➢ Solving an overtrading problem after it occurs is more difficult. It may be necessary to actually turn down business. Raising money may be possible through invoice finance or by finding new investors.
➢ Increasing debt may be difficult if already highly geared. Even if the money can be raised, the terms demanded to quickly fund a large increase in gearing may make the increased sales unprofitable.

Solutions to large amounts of assets:
➢ Working capital is among the many important things that contribute to the success of a business. Without it, a business may cease to function properly or, at all. Not only does a lack of working capital render a company unable to build and grow, but it may also leave a company with too little cash to pay its short-term obligations. Simply put, a company with a very low amount of working capital may be at risk of running out of money.
➢ When a company has too little working capital, it can face financial difficulties and may even be forced towards bankruptcy. This is true of both very small companies and billion-dollar organizations. A company with this problem may pay creditors late or even skip payments. It may borrow money in an attempt to remain afloat. If late payments have affected the company's credit rating, it may have difficulty obtaining a loan at an affordable interest rate.
➢ In some types of businesses, it isn't as much of a problem to have a lower amount of working capital.

Questions:

1. What do you understand by working capital management?
2. Analyse the organization's working capital management.
3. Apart from the solutions provided in the case, suggest some solutions from your side.

A Handbook of Case Studies in Finance
127

21. Sun Light Ltd.: A Case on Capital Budgeting

Sun Light Limited was incorporated on October 17, 1973, as a private limited company, and was converted into a public limited company on November, 15, 1973. The company has been promoted by Shri Babudev Sabarwal and his son, Shri J.P. Sabarwal. The company manufactures ERW steel pipes and tubes, both black and galvanized aluminium alloys, welding heads, GLS lamps, fluorescent tubes and tubular glass shells. The products of the lighting division are sold under the brand name URJA.

In 1986, the company increased the manufacturing capacity of GLS lamps to 15 million per annum, and also set up manufacturing facilities for glass shells for GLS lamps, with a capacity of 30 million per annum. The company embarked on modernisation of the steel tubes division and lighting division, which involved an expenditure of Rs 289 lakhs and 475 lakhs, respectively. It also proposed adding new finishing facilities, expanding the storage area and streamlining the manufacturing flow. On December 14, 1990, the company changed its name from JaiPrakash Tubes Ltd to Sun Light Limited. The steel division not only consolidated its position but also expanded its network geographically.

In 1993, the company set up a joint venture with Sriram GmbH, under the name of Sriram URJA Pvt. Ltd to manufacture the latest energy efficient and innovative lamps. In 1994, the company undertook to set up five new sales offices and introduce new products: 200 W lamp; 500 W lamp; RC lamp; long life incandescent lamp; high pressure mercury vapour lamp; night lamp; decorative lamp; H-3 auto-halogen lamp; and the MR 16 spotlight halogen lamp. The company also undertook the implementation of a ribbon glass shell project in addition to a tube drawing project, lamp cap project, GLS filament project and electrostatic coating machine.

Sun Light has become the leading manufacturer of lighting products in India in less than a decade, but its success has not only been in the domestic market. Rather, Sun Light is also doing well overseas. The lighting division of Sun Light has international standard manufacturing facilities at both its plants at Hameerpur and Pithampur. These ISO 9002 certified, fully integrated plants produce ultra-modern lamps and their components.

Sun Light is the second largest company in the lighting industry. The company has commissioned a state-of-the-art ribbon glass plant in

Pithampur, Gwalior. It has also established URJA Herbal Ltd, a separate company to deal with herbal products.

The directors present the 38th annual report of financial accounts for the year ending March, 31, 2011.

Financial Performance

S. No.	Particulars	F.Y. 2010-2011	F.Y. 2009-2010
1	Turnover	2441.82	1938.93
2	Profit before Interest,	181.93	129.56
3	Depreciation and Taxation (EBIDTA) Interest	60.54	48.71
4	Depreciation	51.24	27.09
5	Profit before tax (PBT)	70.15	53.76
6	Tax Including Deferred Tax	3.42	8.59
7	Profit after taxation(PAT)	66.73	45.17
8	Balance brought forward from the earlier year	154.44	121.76
9	Profit available for appropriations	221.17	166.93
10	Proposed Equity Dividend	6.57	5.57
11	Tax on Distributed Profits	1.06	0.92
12	Transferred to General Reserve	7	6
13	Balance carried to Balance Sheet	206.54	154.44

In the fiscal year under review, the turnover of the company increased to Rs.2441.82 crores from Rs.1938.93 crores in the previous year, registering an increase of 25.94%. The profit after tax increased to Rs. 66.73 crores, as compared to Rs. 45.17 crores in the previous year, registering a growth of 47.73% during this period. The export turnover during the year under review was Rs.275.36 crores, as compared to Rs. 245.45 crores in the previous year.

Case:

Sun Light Ltd is contemplating whether to invest in a new machine, so that the present method of production by manual labour is eliminated. The management has two alternatives, X and Y, in respect of which the following INF Is available:

	Machine X	**Machine Y**
Cost of Machine	150,000	240,000
Estimated Life	5yrs	6yrs
Estimated Savings in Scrap	10,000	15,000
Estimated Cost of Indirect Material	8,000	9,000
Estimated Savings in Direct Wages	90,000	120,000
Additional Cost of Maintenance	5,000	10,000
Additional Cost of Supervision	12,000	16,000

Depreciation may be taken on a straight line method. Assume tax rate of 50%. Sun Light Ltd evaluated the two alternatives by using:

a) Pay-back period method
b) Unadjusted return on average investment method
c) Net present value index method (cost of capital 8%)

22. Big or Small: Financial Loss Matters!

The Rs 2200 crore Sanskar Group is a leading news services group in India with a strong presence in the media industry, entertainment, printing, textiles, fast-moving consumer goods, oils, solvents and internet services. Its media business includes ownership of print media, radio stations and TV channels. The group is the most widely read newspaper group of India with a total readership of Rs 2.67 crores, as per NRS 2006. Its flagship Hindi daily newspaper, Dainik Sanskar, and the Gujarati newspaper, Divya Sanskar, collectively make it the most widely-read daily newspaper. My FM has already launched in Jaipur Chandigarh and Jalandhar, and will soon be available in a total of 17 cities, which would make it the fourth largest FM station network in the country.

Dainik Sanskar was first published in Jabalpur and Gwalior, of the central province. The newspaper was launched in 1966 to fulfil the need for a Hindi language daily. It was launched by Subah in Bhopal and Good Morning Country in Jabalpur, in 1957, and was renamed Sanskar Samachar. In 1968, it was renamed Rozana Sanskar, and it is now the first in India and eleventh in the world for the largest circulation of a daily newspaper. By 1995, Dainik Sanskar had displaced Nayajamana as the number one newspaper in Madhya Pradesh (MP). It set up an in-house team of 700 surveyors. The team was highly trained in customer engagement, and was trained by experts in body language, grooming, posture, approach methods, social norms and rules etc. Based on survey feedback, they went back to each of the households surveyed to show them a prototype of the newspaper and to give them the option to sign up for an advance subscription. The customers were offered a subscription price of Rs. 1.50 (as against the newsstand price of Rs. 2) and a refund in case of dissatisfaction. When Dainik Sanskar's first launched outside MP, on December 19, 1995, it entered the market as the number one newspaper with 172,347 copies. Rajasthan Patrika, the former number one, had a circulation of just 100,000 copies at that time.

Case of Transaction Dispute in Danik Sanskar

Ranvijay joined Danik Sanskar on April 1, 2010 but, for various reasons, was not able to work for more than two months. He resigned from the job and later on (June 1, 2011) he joined another organization. Though he informed the organization's HR department, and the HR manager was aware of this situation, he did not convey his decision concerning his resignation to the finance department. He realised that this department was unaware of his resignation when he noticed that the finance department continued transferring his salary into his account. After the passage of an entire month, the HR manager finally conveyed the information about his resignation to the finance department. But it was too late. They had already transferred one month's salary, with no obligation on the part of the former employee to return it. When the issue came to the attention of the senior VP, he called both the HR and finance manager to account for the blunder.

Questions:

1. Do a SWOT analysis of the organization.
2. Identify and explain the problem in the case.
3. What is the probable solution in this case?
4. What steps should organizations take so that, in the future, such incidences do not occur?

23. Traditional Approach, Limited Promotions: Missed Opportunities

It was a sunny April day in 2014. The afternoon was hot but assistant director of Micro Small Medium Enterprise, Mr Chadokar, was sitting coolly in his chamber at 7 Industrial Area, Tansen Road, Gwalior M.P. India, and was in discussion with two potential entrepreneurs, Mr Jitendra and Mr Nagesh, both from a village in SADA, near Gwalior. They had come to inquire about possible training they wanted to undergo regarding "know how" about ice cream manufacturing. A few days previously, MSME had conducted a training program on this.

MSME is a nationwide, governmental organization working for the development and expansion of manufacturing and service activities within the country. It has district offices to promote the entrepreneurial activities within their areas. It conducts various entrepreneurship development programs, such as skills development for educated and uneducated men and women in the region. Mr Chadokar has been heading the Gwalior office for the last five years and has been a motivating factor for many budding entrepreneurs.

Mr Chadokar: "So young men, what can I do for you?"
Mr Jitendra: [Responding with a gesture and deep sigh] "Sir, we are professionally educated persons working on a salaried job for the last three years, but we are not satisfied with our jobs."
Mr Nagesh: "Sir, we are inclined towards setting up our own business."
Mr Chadokar: "That's great! What kind of business you are looking to set up? Have you identified it?"
Mr Nagesh: "Yes sir, we want to set up an ice cream manufacturing unit, as there seems to be a good demand in the region due to it being such a hot climate."
Mr Jitendra: "We approached a bank to inquire about the procedure and loan requirement. They advised us to meet you at this office."
Mr Chadokar: [With a pleasant smile] "It is good that you have already chosen the business you want to set up. You have made my task easier."
Mr Jitendra: "Sir, we do not have any knowledge about ice cream manufacturing. Can you provide us with some information about the training required for it?"
Mr Chadokar: "We have been conducting training workshops for ice cream manufacturing for the last three months, and the last one for this session completed five days ago."

Mr Nagesh: "Sir, we were not aware of the camp schedule, otherwise we would have definitely got ourselves enrolled."

Mr Chadokar: "We always advertise our programmes in the local newspaper one month before they start; you should have approached us at that time."

Ms Nagesh: "Oh! Unfortunately, we don't have a subscription to the local newspaper. Sir, were the details available online or elsewhere?"

Mr Chadokar: "We don't advertise much. We disseminate information through our already-established networks."

Mr Jitendra: [In a rush] "Sir, please enrol us for the upcoming camp; we are in desperate need of this training."

Mr Chadokar: "For the next few months, we have already decided to run training programs for some other products. For ice cream, you will have to wait for some time now."

Mr Nagesh: "Sir, we want to start our work very soon. Otherwise, summer will be over and we will not find much business!"

Mr Chadokar: "Ok, ok," [passes them a form] "please fill in your details and I will call you if we plan it in future. Sorry for this time."

Mr Jitendra and Mr Nagesh: [about to leave] "Thank you, sir, nice meeting you."

Fifteen minutes later, the phone rang, and Mr Chadokar picked it up with a smile. "Hello?"

Caller: "Sir, I am Devesh, from Bhind."

Mr Chadokar: "Hello Devesh. How may I help you?"

Mr Devesh: "Sir, I want to become an interior designer. Can I get training from MSME?"

Mr Chadokar: "What?! Interior design?!" [shocked at the question, a few seconds of silence] "Sorry, young man, it is not part of our training programs right now."

This was not the first time that Mr Chadokar had encountered not receiving any information about the training programs being conducted by MSME, or of young students asking about skills different from the skills-based training programs. Over the last year, it has become a regular occurrence.

Mr Chadokar was carrying out responsibilities that went beyond those of his job. His approach was of a social worker rather than just a government worker. After being consistently ready and willing to work for the benefit of existing and potential entrepreneurs, he was feeling a sense of dissatisfaction at being unable to work on those issues which were probably out of his control. It was late evening now and he was still wondering what the solution could be.

Questions:

Q1.Critically analyse the case from a marketing perspective.

Q2. Identify the main problem/s in the case.

Q3. Provide some suggestions about improving the promotional approach of MSME.

Q4. What are the upcoming areas in which MSME should start providing training?

TEACHING NOTES

1. **Abstract**: The present case is a narrative and dialogue-based case which gives a clear description of the old-fashioned training programs and obsolete promotional style carried out by MSME. It also talks about the helpless position of the head of the office who wants to work for the benefit of the people who approach him but fails to do so because of the stereotypical workings of the government institution.

2. **Concepts Covered**: The broad areas this case focuses on are entrepreneurship skill development programmes, enterprise initiation, innovation and marketing strategies.

3. **Target Group**: The case can be used for teaching trainees and students of management specializations, for individual analysis. After analysis, the case can be presented individually or in a group. The case is also suitable for written assessment, as well as role play.

4. **Pre-Case Preparations**: The case and reference should be provided to the students at least one day prior to the discussion, for individual analysis.

5. **Generalisation**: The case should be discussed among a small group. The outcome of the small group should be presented in front of the whole class by the representative of the group, in order to evaluate each point in detail. Again, the case can also we left open for group discussion.

6. **Assessment**: The case is suitable for written assessment and oral presentations. The case is even suitable for role play.

7. **References.**

REFERENCES

- GOI. "IRDA ACT 1999". GOI. Retrieved 19 June 2012.
- GOI. "IRDA ACT 1999". Department of Financial Services, GOI. Retrieved 19 June 2012.
- "Lok Sabha passes insurance bill with 4 amendments". 02/12/1999. Rediff News. Retrieved 19 June 2012.
- www.investopedia.com/terms/p/profitabilityratios.asp
- http://www.extension.iastate.edu/agdm/wholefarm/html/c3-24.html
- http://www.investopedia.com/terms/f/financial-account.asp
- Charles P. Kindleberger and Robert Aliber (2005), Manias, Panics, and Crashes: A History of Financial Crises, 5th ed. Wiley, ISBN 0-471-46714-6.
- Luc Laeven and Fabian Valencia (2008), "Systemic banking crises: a new database". International Monetary Fund Working Paper 08/224.
- http://www.investopedia.com/terms/f/financialperformance.asp
- "Audit defined in Six Sigma and Beyond: The Implementation Process Volume VII, D.H. Stamatis (CRC Press, 2002) cited in".
- http://www.investopedia.com/terms/w/workingcapital.asp
- O'Sullivan, Arthur; Sheffrin, Steven M. (2003), Economics: Principles in action. Upper Saddle River, New Jersey 07458: Pearson Prentice Hall. pp. 197, 507. ISBN 0-13-063085-3.
- Bonds, accessed: 2012-06-08
- http://www.legalserviceindia.com/articles/debentures.htm
- "Shares Definition". Investopedia. Retrieved 2013-07-09. http://www.investopedia.com/terms/s/shares.asp
- "Chapter 22 Company-An Introduction". Accountancy. Noida, Uttar Pradesh, India: National Institute of Open Schooling. 2008. p. 242. Retrieved 24 August 2011.
- Hoang, Paul (2007), "1.4 Stakeholders". Business and Management. Victoria: IBID Press. p. 71. ISBN 1-876659-63-7.
- "How to Buy Shares", ShareWorld. Retrieved 23 February 2012.
- http://www.investopedia.com/terms/n/newissue.asp
- *Gregoriou, Greg (2006). Initial Public Offerings (IPOs). Butterworth-Heineman, an imprint of Elsevier. ISBN 0-7506-7975-1.*

- *O'Sullivan, Arthur; Sheffrin, Steven M. (2003). Economics: Principles in Action. Upper Saddle River, NJ: Pearson Prentice Hall. p. 283. ISBN 0-13-063085-3*
- http://www.businessdictionary.com/definition/secondary-market.html
- Frank J. Fabozzi, Steve V. Mann, Moorad Choudhry, The Global Money Markets, Wiley Finance, Wiley and Sons (2002), ISBN 0-471-22093-0.
- Money Market, Investopedia.
  http://www.investopedia.com/university/moneymarket/
- http://finance.mapsofworld.com/capital-market/instruments.html
- Stickney and Weil, 2007, p.791 (Glossary of Financial Accounting: An Intro. to Concepts, Methods, and Use 12e).
- 34 Am. Jur. 2d Federal Taxation ¶ 16762 Section 467 rental agreements defined: "A rental agreement includes any written or oral agreement that provides for the use of tangible property and is treated as a lease for federal income tax purposes".
- It is possible to rent in such a way many things such as domestic animals, electrical appliances, handbags and jewellery. "If, The Observer, 2009-01-04. Retrieved 9 September 2009.
- Diamond, Aubrey (1958). "Advertisements (Hire-Purchase) Act 1957". *Modern Law Review*. Blackwell Publishing. 21 (2). ISSN 0026-7961
- http://www.privco.com/knowledge-bank/private-equity-and-venture-capital
- http://www.investopedia.com/terms/s/seedcapital.asp
- Jerry J. Weygandt; Paul D. Kimmel; Donald E. Kieso (4 May 2010). *Accounting Principles, Peachtree Complete Accounting Workbook.* John Wiley & Sons. p. 60. ISBN 978-0-470-38667-5. Retrieved 6 April 2012.
- Williams, Jan R.; Susan F. Haka; Mark S. Bettner; Joseph V. Carcello (2008). Financial and Managerial Accounting. McGraw-Hill Irwin. p. 40. ISBN 978-0-07-299650-0.
- Sullivan, Arthur; Steven M. Sheffrin (2003), Economics: Principles in action. Upper Saddle River, New Jersey 07458: Pearson Prentice Hall. p. 272. ISBN 0-13-063085-3.
- *"Definition and Recognition of the Elements of Financial Statements" (PDF). Australian Accounting Standards Board. Retrieved 31 March 2015.*
- Kronwald, Christian (2009), Credit Rating and the Impact on Capital Structure. Norderstedt, Germany: Druck und Bingdung. p. 3. ISBN 978-3-640-57549-7.

- Signoriello, Vincent J. (1991), *Commercial Loan Practices and Operations*, ISBN 978-1-55520-134-0
- http://business.gov.in/starting_business/org_private_ltd.php
- http://www.investopedia.com/terms/r/ratioanalysis.asp
- http://www.investopedia.com/terms/p/profitabilityratios.asp
- http://www.investopedia.com/terms/l/liquidityratios.asp
- http://www.accountingcoach.com/financial-ratios/explanation
- http://www.investopedia.com/terms/m/marketcapitalization.asp
- *Roos, Alexander; Khanna, Dinesh; Verma, Sharad; Lang, Nikolaus; Dolya, Alex; Nath, Gaurav; Hammoud, Tawfik. "Getting More Value from Joint Ventures". Transaction Advisors. ISSN 2329-9134*
- Marcos Antonio Mendoza, "Reinsurance as Governance: Governmental Risk Management Pools as a Case Study in the Governance Role Played by Reinsurance Institutions", 21 Conn. Ins. L.J. 53, (2014) http://papers.ssrn.com/sol3/papers.cfm?abstract_id=2573253
- https://www.moneysmart.gov.au/tools-and-resources/calculators-and-apps/budget-planner
- http://www.iso.org/iso/home/store/catalogue_tc/catalogue_detail.htm?csnumber=43033
- www.sbilife.co.in/sbilife/content/11_3483
- "History of Demat". Kotak Securities. Retrieved 18 February 2015
- http://web.archive.org/web/20101003235606/http://www.sebi.gov.in/sebiweb/stpages/about_sebi.jsp
- http://www.investopedia.com/terms/d/depository.asp
- "SEBI registered Depository Participants of CSDL as on 29-02-2012", Securities and Exchange Board of India. Retrieved 16 February 2014.
- "SEBI registered Depository Participants of NSDL as on 31-01-2012", Securities and Exchange Board of India. Retrieved 16 February 2014.
- http://www.investopedia.com/terms/p/portfolio.asp
- "Financial Services: Getting the Goods". IMF. 28 March 2012. Retrieved 8 September 2015
- Marx, Karl, "A Contribution to the Critique of Political Economy", contained in the Collected Works of Karl Marx and Frederick Engels: Volume 29 (International Publishers: New York, 1987) p. 269.
- Marx, Karl, "Outlines of the Critique of Political Economy (Rough Draft of 1857-1857)", contained in the Collected Works of Karl Marx and Frederick Engels: Volume 28 (International Publishers: New York, 1986) p. 80.
- https://www.csi.ca/student/en_ca/designations/cswp.xhtml

- *Ferris, Paul (1984). Gentlemen of Fortune: The World's Merchant and Investment Bankers. London: Weidenfeld and Nicolson. ISBN 0-297-78380-7.*
- "U.S. Securities and Exchange Commission Information on Mutual Funds". U.S. Securities and Exchange Commission (SEC). Retrieved 4 June 2011.
- Lemke, Lins and Smith, Regulation of Investment Companies (Matthew Bender, 2014 ed.).
- Lemke, Lins, Hoenig and Rube, Hedge Funds and Other Private Funds: Regulation and Compliance (Thomson West, 2014-2015 ed.).
- United States Patent and Trademark Office (uspto.gov), Trademark Electronic Search System (TESS). Serial number 74404471.
- Vaughan, E. J., 1997, *Risk Management*, New York: Wiley.
- http://www.investopedia.com/terms/w/wacc.asp
- http:// Joshua M. Pearce. (2015) Return on Investment for Open Source Hardware Development. *Science and Public Policy*. DOI: 10.1093/scipol/scv034 open access
- Joshua M. Pearce. (2015) Return on Investment for Open Source Hardware Development. *Science and Public Policy*. DOI: 10.1093/scipol/scv034 open access
- http://www.investopedia.com/terms/r/returnonassets.asp
- http://www.investopedia.com/terms/c/cagr.asp
- Needles, Belverd E., Marian Powers, Susan V. Crosson (2010), Financial and Managerial Accounting, p. 373.
- Damodaran, Aswath. "Acquisitions and Takeovers". Transaction Advisors. ISSN 2329-9134
- http://www.inventoryops.com/economic_order_quantity.htm
- Armstrong, Scott, Fred Collopy, Andreas Graefe and Kesten C. Green, "Answers to Frequently Asked Questions". Retrieved 15 May, 2013.
- Sullivan, Arthur; Steven M. Sheffrin (2005), Economics: Principles in action. Upper Saddle River, New Jersey 07458: Pearson Prentice Hall. p. 375. ISBN 0-13-063085-3.
- Scrapyard Metal Prices and Auctions: Worldwide Metal Prices and News Website
- Moneyterms.co.uk. NOPAT
- investopedia.com. NOPAT
- Impact of just-in-time (JIT) inventory system on efficiency, quality and flexibility among manufacturing sector, small and medium enterprise (SMEs) in South Africa, Musara Mazanai, African Journal of Business Management Vol. 6(17), pp. 5786-5791, 2 May, 2012, pp.5787-5788.

- Street's Weather: Bonus Showers - WSJ.com